D0393083

EXCELLENCE
IN
SEED, TIME, AND HARVEST

By Robb Thompson

Unless otherwise indicated, all Scripture quotations are taken from the *New King James Version,* copyright © 1982 by Thomas Nelson, Inc. All rights reserved.

Scripture quotations marked *KJV* are taken from the *King James Version* of the Bible.

Scripture quotations marked *AMP* are taken from *The Amplified Bible. Old Testament* copyright © 1965, 1987 by Zondervan Corporation, Grand Rapids, Michigan. *New Testament* copyright © 1958, 1987 by The Lockman Foundation, La Habra, California. All rights reserved.

Scripture quotations marked *NIV* are taken from the *Holy Bible: New International Version®. NIV®.* Copyright © 1973, 1978, 1984 by International Bible Society. Used by permission of Zondervan Publishing House. All rights reserved.

Scripture quotations marked *TLB* are taken from *The Living Bible,* copyright © 1971. Used by permission of Tyndale House Publishers, Inc., Wheaton, Illinois. All rights reserved.

Scripture quotations marked *NAS* are taken from *The New American Standard Bible.* Copyright © 1960, 1962, 1963, 1968, 1971, 1972, 1973, 1975, 1977 by the Lockman Foundation. All rights reserved.

Scripture quotations marked *NLT* are taken from the *New Living Translation.* Copyright © 1996 by Tyndale Charitable Trust, Wheaton, Illinois. All rights reserved.

Excellence in Seed, Time, and Harvest
ISBN 1-889723-39-8
Copyright © 2003 by Robb Thompson
Family Harvest Church
18500 92nd Ave.
Tinley Park, Illinois 60477

Editorial Consultant: Cynthia Hansen
Cover Design: Greg Lane

Printed in the United States of America.
All rights reserved under International Copyright Law.
Contents and/or cover may not be reproduced in whole or in part in any form without the express written consent of the Publisher.

A SPECIAL THANK YOU TO THESE *WINNING IN LIFE* PARTNERS FOR HELPING ME TAKE THIS BOOK AROUND THE WORLD:

Phyllis Abernathy
Myrna Abrian
Mark & Colleen Aitkenhead
Walter & Anna Aldape
Renee Andreasen
Mary Arrigoni
Larry Baston
Darryl Bell
Barbara Bentley
John & Kim Berberich
Anthony & Vendetta Blowe
Doug & Markay Boettcher
Michael, Alana, & Bryan Boettcher
Rosemary Boggs
Cheryl Bonnet
Martricia Bowers
Jean Brigman
Michael & Yvounda Brown
Audrey Bullard
Ray & Gloria Burton
William & Joyce Butler
William Butler, Jr.
Steven & Lorna Carrara
Crosby & Kaylene Carson
Joshua Carson
Tom & Elise Case
Gwen Chaffen
MaryAnn Cherry
Penny Christian
Michael & Rose Clancy
Ron & Tamaraollum
Jerry & Amy Cortez
Sheri Crosby
David & Vonya Currey
Joy De Shazer
Mark & Mary Dempsey
Steve & Christine De Young
Nicole Dillon
Jeanine Donner
Nathaniel & Leola Douglas
Wendy Durham
Marsha Easter
William Elliott
Joseph Ewing

Greg Fagiano
Rich Farm
Susan Faro
Madeline Figueroa
Rich & Marge Flores
Glenn & Thea Fox
Darren & Mary Freihage
Adrienne Fry
Jesus Galban
Trent Gaston
Trent Gaston
Angela Gayden
Paul & Pam Geallis
Nathan & Connie Giffin
Karen Gilgenberg
Larry & Kitty Gill
Jill Grahovec
Joseph Green
William & Rosalie Green
Helena Greenfield
Kris Griffiths
Jacqueline Guerra
Keith & Denise Gunter
Mary Joan Gunther
Robin Hampton
Wannipha Harlow
Rhonda Harr
Walter & Jacqueline Kaye
    Harrington
Sonya Harris
Eddie & Sissy Hartsell
Ed & Deanna Hauschild
Eileen Hawkins
Arlene Henderson
Greg & Stephanie Henthorn
Drew & Sue Hickey
Rhiannon Hickey
Leroy & Landau Hicks
Shirley Holman
Ed Holt
Keri Hooper
Ruby Hougham
Al & Sandra Houston
Carl & Deborah Johnson

Patrice Johnson
Albert Jones
Billy Junkunc
Marlyn Kaufman
Douglas Keessen
Mark & Sharon Killacky
Andy & Mary Knapp
Thomas & Michelle Lally
Phil & Mary Lambert
John Lapinski
Erskine & Rosalyn Leonard
Phyllis Leonardo
Glenn & Angelia Leszczak
Loretta Levin
Joe Linder
Dorothy Lowe
Keli Loyd
Hosea & Lohmia Lyles
Bruce Mac Ritchie
Gail Mallett
Steve & Sherise Marinich
John & Ana Luisa Martinez
Anna Marie Martusciello
Geri Maslan
Gale & Elizabeth Mathus
Deborah Mc Clanahan
Ken & Lori Mc Graw
Margaret Mc Guire
Velda McNitt
Benjamin & Sandra Medina
Janice Michalec
Felicia Middlebrooks
Frank & Joanne Miller
Felicia Moore
Lyle & Charmaine Moore
Tonya Moore
Thomas & Anna Nestor
Thomas Nestor, Jr
Stephen & Rhonda Osborn
Michael Paledino
Javier & Julia Palos
Darryl & Carla Parque
Stacey Patterson
Joe & Sue Petrovic
James & Margaret Phaby
William Plut
Fred & Betty Postma
Robert & Mary Beth Pozdol
Deborah Pruett
James & Doris Quigley

Misy Read
Johnmark & Patty Ridings
Frances Robinson
Patrick & Sonya Robinson
William & Regina Robinson
Frank & Isabell Romanazzi
Cary & Patrici Rosenbaum
Richard & Diane Rozich
Frances Rudolph
William Rudolph
George & Jennifer San Jose
Eugene & Gilda Santor
Daniel & Kiana Savage
Gail Schultz
Todd Schultz
Jae Seo
Warren & Linda Shafer
Sanford & Nancy Shannon
Steve & Megan Shapiro
Chris & Cindy Shefts
John Smith
Kitty Snyder Nemec
Serge & Marilyn Sokol
Michelle Solis
Holly Stasiak
Emily Stinnett
Dan Stinnett
Susan Stinnett
Patricia Styles
Katherine Surbaugh
Ray & Stephanie Tamayo
Diana Taylor
Barry Thomas
Deron & Tiffany Thomas
Sheila Thomas
William & Peggy Vander Velde
Phyllis Vickery
Mark & Lisa Voightmann
Dwayne & Mogda Walker
Richard & Bette Wagner
Dino & Monica White
Greg & Angie Wiggins
Karen Wilkins
Chuck & Melody Willett
Torran & Linda Williams
Derek & Cynthia Wilson
Nancy Wimberly
Sylvia Winfrey
Telie Woods
Melissa Woodward

TABLE OF CONTENTS

Acknowledgments

Introduction

ACKNOWLEDGMENTS

I owe all that I know on this subject to three wonderful forerunners in the Body of Christ: Peter Daniels (my father who adopted me); Dr. John Avanzini; and Dr. Mike Murdock.

Your input in my life has been immeasurable and has given me definition for life. Thank you. I could never repay you for your kindness.

INTRODUCTION

I don't know about you, but I want a Christianity that is real in every area of my life. I'm not interested in a belief system that only works inside the church walls. I want something that works at the gas station too! I want to be able to buy a new car with money, not with faith, because I haven't met a car dealer yet who accepts faith as payment for the car I want to buy!

I'm so grateful that God has never disappointed me. I've learned over the years that His desire is for us to advance in every arena, including the financial realm. To that end, He has given us principles to follow and promises to claim in His Word.

In this book, I want to share with you some of the excellence principles of giving and prosperity that have helped changed my life from one of utter defeat to a daily experience of victory. You see, I come from a background of welfare, eviction, alcoholism, drug addiction, and witchcraft. All these strongholds were in my immediate family line. There was just no way in the world I was going to get out of my predetermined destiny on my own. The devil had already set the course of my life. He had been working for generations to secure my failure through the sins and wrong choices of my forefathers.

Then I got saved and everything changed. In the spiritual realm, old things passed away and all things became new (2 Cor. 5:17). However, in the natural, my life was still messed up. And even though I was a new creature in Christ, I had no clue what I needed to do to get my life in order and move up to a higher level.

So I did the only thing I knew to do — I went to the Bible to find out what God said about every area of life — including this area of finances. I didn't care what *I* thought about anything. I was only interested in learning what *God* thinks.

In the Word I discovered a secret Holy Ghost weapon that caused me to turn out differently than the rest of my family — the pursuit of excellence according to the Word of God. This same weapon is available to all of us, and it will take us to a higher level of life than we ever imagined.

So keep in mind as you read on — I didn't come up with these principles on my own. Every one of these principles of giving and prosperity that I'm about to share with you can be found in God's Word. However, I *have* proven the truth of these excellence principles in my own life. In fact, I have advanced in my life and ministry far beyond my wildest dreams.

Of course, even people in the world go out each day and do what they can to make more money and advance in life. But here is the difference between people in the world and me: They are striving to advance for *themselves*; I want to advance so I can help *other people*. I am well aware that I can't give to others what I don't have. Therefore, I continually want to increase in finances so I can increase in giving. My goal is that once you have read this book, you will want the same thing too.

Please understand that I'm not writing this book to give you a Bible story; I'm writing it to give you a priceless opportunity. I want to tell you what has changed my life in this area of finances so *your* life can be changed for the better as well. I know it's nice to hear about someone else who has been blessed, but it isn't enough. If you aren't seeing increase in your own life, there will always be something on the inside of you that asks, *Lord, when is it going to happen for me?*

I'm telling you, you *can* experience an absolute turnaround in your finances. You can change your socioeconomic destiny and greatly bless others in the process. All you have to do is pursue excellence in giving according to this key principle: *Just as the harvest never comes before the time of sowing, the blessing of the Lord never comes before the seed.*

I can tell you this from personal experience — there is absolutely nothing more fulfilling in life than to jump headlong into this particular pursuit. You can rise to greater heights in God than you have ever imagined just by learning how to activate the *power of the seed*!

Robb Thompson

★ ★ ★ ★ ★

CHAPTER ONE

GOD'S WILL FOR OUR FINANCES

What is God's will concerning the finances of His people? This is a difficult thing for many Christians to understand. They may talk about the tithe or about giving offerings to the Lord, but they don't really realize what God says in His Word concerning their prosperity.

Psalm 35:27 sums up God's perspective on this subject in a nutshell:

> **Let them shout for joy and be glad, who favor my righteous cause; and let them say continually, "Let the Lord be magnified, who has pleasure in the prosperity of His servant."**

The *Moffatt's* translation says that God **"...loves to see His servant prospering."**[1] This is God's will concerning your finances, and later I'll show you many other scriptures to prove it. You're going to find out how you

---

[1] James Moffatt, *A New Translation of the Bible* (New York and London: Harper and Brothers Publishers, 1935), p.xx.

can advance in life according to the Word so you can enjoy the prosperity God intends for you to enjoy!

Learning How To Be Poor

It seems ironic to me that the only people I've ever met who *don't* believe they should consciously pursue financial advancement in life are those who call themselves believers. I first discovered this many years ago when I got saved and started associating with Christians. Almost immediately, my newfound friends began to teach me how to be poor.

I didn't know how to do that at the time. When I was still a messed-up sinner, I worked at a business in downtown Chicago and made very good money. I had done everything I could, both ethically and sometimes unethically, to make sure I lived well.

Then in 1975 I came to Christ in a mental institution — and I'm telling you, when I got saved, I got saved! At midnight on October 28, 1975, I went to sleep as a man who wanted to die. On October 29, I woke up as a brand-new person. I didn't really understand what had happened, but I knew it was something that had changed my life forever. (You can read a detailed account of my story in my book, *The Great Exchange: Your Thoughts for God's Thoughts.*)

But the fellow who led me to the Lord was from a denomination that did not teach or believe in prosperity. In fact, that particular denomination teaches that material wealth somehow makes a person less spiritual than poverty does.

These were the only Christians I knew in my early days as a believer. I thought everyone who was saved belonged to that denomination! I wouldn't trade my experience with those believers for anything. They gave me a great foundation in the Word of God regarding my salvation. However, beyond that basic foundation, they couldn't teach me anything.

As a new Christian, I learned from my fellow believers that I needed to learn how to be content and "make do" the best I could with what I had. They taught me to avoid expecting anything from God because "we never know what the Lord is going to do." Therefore, instead of seeing my financial situation get better after my initial experience with the Lord, it actually got much worse.

My Christians friends took me to their little Christian clubs that teach families how to stretch their dollar and live on a very low grocery budget. I must admit, those people came up with some inventive ways to make a nice meal with very little to work with. They almost seemed to perform a miracle every time they cooked dinner!

So I became a part of the "Christian poverty club." This new mentality made me feel a little like a freak, but at least I was happy in Jesus! I was just so thankful that the Lord would allow me to hang around the doors of His sanctuary and spend time praising Him. If I had to live in poverty to serve Him, I reasoned, it was worth it.

Then I learned that God doesn't like people to drive nice cars. The people at church told me, "Good Christians don't drive Corvettes."

Well, I owned a Chevrolet Corvette! So I prayed and said, "Lord, this Corvette has to get out of here because I'm a Christian, and I love You more than I love it. So one of two things has to happen: Either You need to sell my car, or You need to have someone steal it."

Now, keep in mind that I had only been a Christian for a few weeks, so I didn't really know that God doesn't tell people to steal. I just prayed according to what I knew — and the next day, someone stole my Corvette!

When I found out, I thought, *Praise the Lord!* Then I called Linda at work and said, "Honey, did you see the Corvette parked outside when you went to work today?"

She replied, "No, I don't remember seeing it. But actually, I don't remember not seeing it either."

"Linda, someone stole it!" I exclaimed happily.

Linda (who was also a brand-new Christian) started jumping up and down and screaming about how happy she was that the car had been stolen. Her coworkers couldn't believe it. Earlier they had concluded she must be off her rocker to become a Christian in the first place. Now they *knew* she was off her rocker! Who in their right mind would jump up and down with joy because their spouse's car had just been stolen?

Both Linda and I were extremely ignorant at the time about this subject of prosperity in the life of a Christian. But I'll show you how sincere I was about that prayer I prayed. When the insurance company wanted to settle with me, they offered me a particular amount of money, but I told them I wouldn't take it.

"Why won't you take it?" the insurance representative asked.

"Because it's too much," I replied.

"Mr. Thompson, are you saying that we're offering you *too much* for your car?"

"That's right."

"Are you going to take this money?"

"No," I said firmly.

You see, I had lived a life of dishonesty, and I wanted to be pure before God. Therefore, I refused to look at a dime that didn't belong to me.

But the insurance woman said to me, "Look, Mr. Thompson, I'm going to give it to you straight. If you don't take this check, it will take too much time to reprocess the payment and give you the amount of money you want. So, please, you just have to take this check!"

So I reluctantly took the insurance check. However, I cried as I did it because my desire to take nothing that wasn't mine was so strong in me.

Then something happened to change my thinking about living a life of just "making do." I had a conversation with a friend of mine named Joe.

Joe was a very nice man who had done very well for himself financially. He and his wife had graciously looked in on Linda daily while I was in the mental institution.

One day I saw him and said, "Joe, I want to talk to you."

He said, "Robb, you can say anything you want to say to me about Jesus for ten minutes."

So I began to witness to Joe. I told him everything I knew about Jesus — which didn't even take the entire ten minutes!

Then Joe looked at me and asked, "Robb, why would I want to receive Jesus?"

"What do you mean?" I asked.

"Well, look at you," Joe replied. "When you went into the looney bin, there was nothing wrong with you. You might have been a little confused, but you worked in downtown Chicago. You made a lot of money. You lived well. You ate well. You were respected. People wanted to be around you. Now you're coming to me and telling me that I need Jesus. Why would I want to believe that? Just look at your life now, and then look at mine."

I couldn't think of a thing to say to Joe in reply. After all, the prosperous lifestyle he was talking about was the very thing I had been told was wrong.

I realized something at that moment:

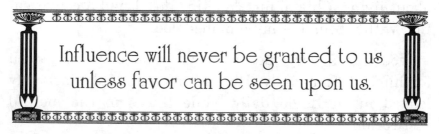

Influence will never be granted to us unless favor can be seen upon us.

Even though I had said all the right words to Joe, I couldn't attract him to the Gospel message because, as far as he knew from observing my life, Jesus was a poor Man when He walked on this earth.

I didn't know it at the time, but all I needed was one verse to clear up that misunderstanding. I'm talking about what Jesus said in John 12:8:

"For the poor you have with you always, but Me you do not have always."

That's a simple but very profound verse. With just a few words, Jesus made a distinction between Himself and the poor. He was saying in essence, "The poor will be around forever, but I'm only going to be here a little while. So pour on the expensive ointment. Be extravagant in living your life for Me."

Jesus understood something we all need to understand:

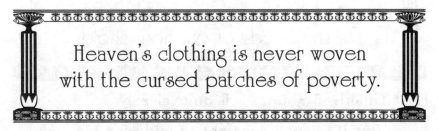

Heaven's clothing is never woven with the cursed patches of poverty.

That's why I want to go through the Scriptures and show you what God's will is concerning your finances. I want to share some principles of excellence that, when followed, will absolutely change your socioeconomic destiny in this life.

I know I'm speaking the truth because this is exactly what *I* did. The principles I discuss in this book aren't just a bunch of theories to me. I'm not just relating a nice little Bible story that sounds good. I'm telling you, *you CAN change your future on purpose — just because you want to.* The key lies in how diligent you are to pursue excellence in the area of giving.

Why God Wants Us To Prosper

After my conversation with Joe, I decided to go to the Word without a preconceived opinion so I could discover what God's will is concerning my finances. I began to see that what God believes about the subject is the very opposite of what most Christians believe.

The Bible actually gives us many reasons why God *wants* His people to prosper.

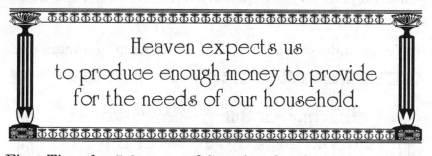

Heaven expects us
to produce enough money to provide
for the needs of our household.

First Timothy 5:8 states this quite clearly:

> **But if anyone does not provide for his own, and especially for those of his household, he has denied the faith and is worse than an unbeliever.**

Someone might ask, "Do you mean that if I don't provide for the material needs of my immediate family, I am actually denying the faith? I don't think that's true."

Sure, it's true. Remember, I didn't say it; *God* said it. But people aren't used to hearing someone teach on what God says in that particular scripture.

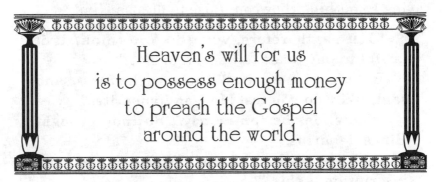

Heaven's will for us is to possess enough money to preach the Gospel around the world.

We're not supposed to just take up space until we go home to be with Jesus.

The Bible says in Romans 10:14 and 15, "**...And how shall they hear without a preacher? And how shall they preach unless they are sent?...**" Well, how are preachers sent around the world to preach the Gospel? *With money.*

God wants me to have enough money to be able to send people to preach the Gospel. That's the reason I have no trouble giving offerings to missions — because I'm not called to go myself! The Hyatt Regency is about as rugged as it gets for me. But there are people who love ministering on the mission field. I think that's great — and I'm glad to help send them by giving freely of my finances!

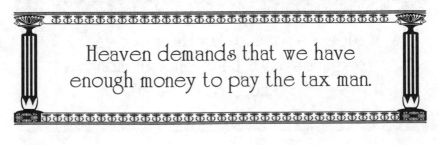

Heaven demands that we have enough money to pay the tax man.

As amazing as it may seem, Christians do cheat on their taxes. But look at what Jesus said about this subject when the Pharisees tried to trick Him into saying something they could use to accuse Him:

> "Tell us, therefore, what do You think? Is it lawful to pay taxes to Caesar, or not?"
> But Jesus perceived their wickedness, and said, "Why do you test Me, you hypocrites?
> "Show Me the tax money." So they brought Him a denarius.
> And He said to them, "Whose image and inscription is this?"
> They said to Him, "Caesar's." And He said to them, "Render therefore to Caesar the things that are Caesar's, and to God the things that are God's."
>
> **Matthew 22:17-21**

Jesus just told us two things in verse 21: 1) We are to pay our taxes, and 2) we are to tithe.

In our day, "Caesar" has found a way to require a substantial portion of our income in the form of federal and state taxes. Nevertheless, I obey the words of Jesus and pay unto Caesar what belongs to him — but not a penny more!

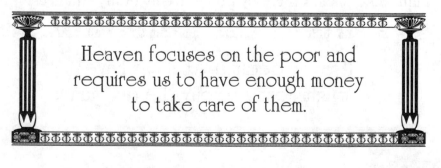

Heaven focuses on the poor and requires us to have enough money to take care of them.

Look at what Proverbs 19:17 says about this:

He who has pity on the poor lends to the Lord, and He will pay back what he has given.

Notice that this verse doesn't have the same message as Luke 6:38. It doesn't say that *men* will give back to you "pressed down, shaken together, and running over" according to what you have given to the poor.

There is a good reason for this. You see, when you have pity on the poor, you are not sowing seed that God can multiply into a larger harvest. Why is that? Because the poor have nothing to give back. You cannot sow a seed in ground that cannot produce. Therefore, *God* is going to pay back the money you give to the poor. Then you will be able to sow that money into good, fruit-producing ground.

Personally, I never sow into a dead end, so I don't sow into poverty. Rather, I give to the poor, and I make sure I give generously. I give to feed the poor. I give to missions organizations that minister to the poor. But I save my seed to sow into good ground that will produce a multiplied harvest.

The list of reasons that God wants us to have money is beginning to add up, isn't it? The truth is, I could give you many more reasons why God wants us to have money. But remember this:

Heaven's requirements
never precede Heaven's provisions.

Whether God gives us twelve or twenty reasons why He wants us to have money, He has already provided enough money for us to fulfill every one of those reasons. Philippians 4:19 (*KJV*) says, **"But my God shall supply ALL of your need according to His riches in glory by Christ Jesus."**

I want us to review these basic principles one more time:

1. Heaven expects us to produce enough money to provide for the needs of our household.

2. Heaven's will for us is to possess enough money to preach the Gospel around the world.

3. Heaven demands that we have enough money to pay the tax man.

4. Heaven focuses on the poor and requires us to have enough money to take care of them.

5. Heaven's requirements never precede Heaven's provisions.

Now let's take a moment to pray before we go further to find out what God has to say about our prosperity.

Father, we thank You that You have hidden these truths from the greedy and revealed them to the sincere. May the eyes of our understanding be enlightened so that we would know the hope to which You have called us. Change us by Your Word as we seek out its truth, for it is a lamp unto our feet and a light unto our path. In Jesus' Name, amen.

What God Says About Our Prosperity

There are many people who visit local churches with miracle ministries and healing ministries. Many others come through and teach believers about righteousness. But there needs to be much more teaching about money. Why? Because money is what believers need, even more than they need to be healed.

We need money every day; we *don't* need to be healed every day. Every day there is money going out of our bank accounts. Every moment we take a breath, it's costing us money. Every time we wake up in the morning, we have to pay for that night's stay in the place where we laid our heads. Everything we own cost us something, and the meter just keeps on running. Therefore, money is what we need more than anything else in this natural life.

Second Timothy 3:16,17 says, **"All Scripture is given by inspiration of God, and is profitable for doctrine, for reproof, for correction, for instruction in righteousness, that the man of God may be complete, thoroughly equipped for every good work."** Being thoroughly equipped for every good work includes having the necessary money to carry out God's will. Therefore, we need to be instructed in what God has to say in His Word about our prosperity.

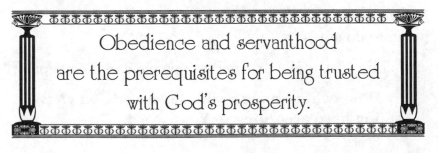

Obedience and servanthood are the prerequisites for being trusted with God's prosperity.

We looked earlier at Psalm 35:27, which says that God *takes pleasure* in our prosperity. But is that truth borne out throughout the Bible? It most assuredly is. Let's look at a few more scriptures that reveal God's will for our finances.

Job 36:11 says this:

If they [the righteous] **obey and serve Him, they shall spend their days in prosperity, and their years in pleasures.**

If we obey and serve God, we will spend our days in prosperity and our years in pleasure. Now I don't know about you, but that's what I want! But if we're *not* spending our days in prosperity and our years in pleasure, that means we're either not obeying God or we're not serving Him in some area of our lives.

Therefore, we just have to keep two things on our minds in order to enjoy abundance and prosperity in life: 1) obedience and 2) servanthood. When we fulfill these two requirements, all of a sudden two things happen: 1) we begin to prosper and 2) God is pleased.

Once we truly understand this principle, we'll stop putting God's integrity on the line by wondering whether or not He will come through for us. Instead, we'll focus on making sure *we* come through for *Him*. We already know what God is going to do. The question is, are we going to do *our* part?

Psalm 119:9 tells us exactly how we can do our part:

How can a young man cleanse his way? By taking heed according to Your word.

If we will just stick to the Word of God, rebellion and bad habits will begin to fall off our lives and obedience will come to the forefront. Our desire will be to serve the Lord. Then we will spend our days in prosperity and our years in pleasure as we "take heed according to His Word."

I'm excited about that! God said if I will fulfill His requirements according to His Word, blessings are mine!

Now look at Job 8:7 (*NAS*): **"Though your beginning was insignificant, yet your end will increase greatly."** *The Jerusalem Bible* says it this way: **"Your former state will seem to you as nothing beside your new prosperity."**[2] Get hold of this scripture, because that's God's will for *you*!

Certainly this scripture came to pass in the lives of God's people when the Lord freed them from slavery under the Egyptian Pharaoh's harsh rule. The Israelite's former state of slavery must have seemed as nothing beside their new prosperity, for the Bible says that God **"...brought them out with silver and gold, and there was none feeble among His tribes"** (Ps. 105:37).

In Psalm 23:1, David tells us that God never wants one need to go unmet in our lives: **"The Lord is my shepherd; I shall not want."** *The Living Bible* puts it this way: **"Because the Lord is my Shepherd, I have everything I need!"**

Psalm 34:9,10 echoes this truth:

> **Oh, fear the Lord, you His saints! There is no want to those who fear Him.**

---

[2] *The Jerusalem Bible* (New York: Darton, Longman, and Todd, Ltd., and Doubleday Publishers, 1966), p.xx.

The young lions lack and suffer hunger; but those who seek the Lord shall not lack any good thing.

Now look at the way these verses read in *The Living Bible:*

If you belong to the Lord, reverence him; for everyone who does this has everything he needs.
Even strong young lions sometimes go hungry, but those of us who reverence the Lord will never lack any good thing.

I also like the *Amplified* translation of verse 10:

...They who seek (inquire of and require) the Lord [by right of their need and on the authority of His Word], none of them shall lack any beneficial thing.

God gives an awesome promise for the righteous man to claim in Psalm 112:3: "**Wealth and riches will be in his house, and his righteousness endures forever.**" *The Living Bible* says, "**He himself shall be wealthy....**"

Then Proverbs 8:21 says something very interesting about God's desire for the righteous man to prosper:

I [wisdom] **traverse the way of righteousness, in the midst of the paths of justice, that I may cause those who love me to inherit wealth, that I may fill their treasuries.**

This is wisdom speaking now. Wisdom is saying, "God will cause those who love Him to inherit wealth." But where is that wealth going to come from? It won't come from your natural job. That's why your most important job is to pursue *God*. You have to determine, "I'm going to pursue God — every day, every day, *every day*. Meanwhile, I know that God will cause my answer to come to me!"

I encourage you to confess on a regular basis, "Because I love wisdom, I excel in my work. I will stand before great men, not obscure men, because wisdom is the principal thing. I will get wisdom, and with all my getting, I will get understanding."

Someone may say, "Now wait a minute — do you mean to tell me that if I love the Word of God and the wisdom of God, He will fill my treasuries as He causes me to inherit wealth? Then why is it that I don't know very many Christians with full treasuries?"

The answer is simple: Either God is lying, or we need to rise to another level of excellence in the realm of finances. Personally, I'm not going to be the one to call God a liar. Romans 3:4 says, **"...Let God be true but every man a liar..."** — and that includes me!

Proverbs 10:22 is a wonderful promise for us to claim: **"The blessing of the Lord makes one rich, and He adds no sorrow with it."** But there is a condition to this promise, and it is found in Proverbs 11:24,25:

> There is one who scatters, yet increases more; and there is one who withholds more than is right, but it leads to poverty.
> The generous soul will be made rich, and he who waters will also be watered himself.

Notice that verse 24 *doesn't* say that the second person didn't give at all. It says that he withheld more than he should have withheld. Everyone else may have thought that this person was a giver and therefore wondered why the Word wasn't working in his life. Well, these verses clear up the confusion. The person who withholds more than he should is heading toward poverty, but the generous person will be made rich.

Proverbs 13:22 is a scripture that most of us are familiar with. It says this:

A good man leaves an inheritance to his children's children, but the wealth of the sinner is stored up for the righteous.

Christians love to claim this divine promise, but let me tell you something that is important for you to understand about this verse. God is *not* going to take wealth away from the diligent and give it to the lazy. I can prove that statement with Proverbs 10:4:

He who has a slack hand becomes poor, but the hand of the diligent makes rich.

That's why I like the *Amplified* version of Proverbs 13:22, which stresses God's requirement of godly character in order to receive the promise:

A good man leaves an inheritance [of moral stability and goodness] to his children's children, And the wealth of the sinner [finds its way eventually] into the hands of the righteous, for whom it was laid up.

The following verses also emphasize the condition of godly character and obedience in order to enjoy God's promise of prosperity:

By humility and the fear of the Lord are riches and honor and life.

Proverbs 22:4

If you are willing and obedient, you will eat the best from the land.

Isaiah 1:19 *NIV*

I like the way *The Living Bible* paraphrases Isaiah 1:19: **"If you will only let me help you, if you will only obey, then I will make you rich!"**

I want to share one more scripture that reveals God's will regarding our prosperity. Isaiah 61:7 (*AMP*) tells us that whatever the devil has stolen from us in the past, God desires to give back to us a twofold recompense:

Instead of your [former] shame you shall have a twofold recompense; instead of dishonor and reproach [your people] shall rejoice in their portion. Therefore in their land they shall possess double [what they had forfeited]; everlasting joy shall be theirs.

You may say, "I love what the Scriptures have to say about prosperity. But how do I begin to live this life of abundance that God desires for me?"

That's what we're going to talk about in the following chapters. I don't want you to live out your entire life at the same financial level, always just scraping by from one paycheck to the next. I'm determined to help you rise with me to a higher level in life!

The Consequences
Of Refusing To Listen

If all those prosperity scriptures we just looked at are true, why is it that most Christians don't have enough money to do what God requires of them?

I used to ask God that question a lot. I couldn't stand the fact that many of the people I had fellowshipped with at one time in my life were no longer qualified for my time because they weren't possessing the portion God had already given to them. I was bothered that while God was changing me, they always seemed to stay the same.

So I began to think, *What have I been doing differently than these other people? Why have I continued to rise to new levels of increase and blessing while they've stayed in the same place, defeated and discouraged, year after year?*

Hosea 4:6 holds a clue to the reason so many Christians live their entire lives in defeat: **"My people are destroyed for lack of knowledge...."** That word "destroyed" can also be translated "devoured." In other words, when God's people lack the knowledge they need to obey His principles, the devourer is not being rebuked in their lives and they are left open to attack.

However, it's important to realize that there are two kinds of ignorance. The first kind arises from a lack of knowledge or a lack of understanding about a particular subject. The second kind of ignorance results from choosing to ignore or refusing to listen to knowledge already gained.

God is talking about this second kind of ignorance in this scripture. He goes on to say, **"...Because you have rejected knowledge, I also will reject you from being priest for Me; because you have forgotten the law of your God, I also will forget your children."**

Notice that the people's lack of knowledge was based on their rejection of God's truth. God's response to that rejection was strong. He said, "Because you have rejected My knowledge, I will reject you. You will no longer be priests unto Me. And because you have forgotten the law of your God, I will forget your children."

If we want our children to be blessed, we better take heed to what God is saying here about not ignoring His Word!

When I read that verse, I thought, *Wait a minute! That means our children will actually have to deal with the things we refused to deal with in our lives!*

Think about it. If we're honest with ourselves, we have to admit that we've had to deal with sins, faults, and strongholds in our own lives that our parents never dealt with in *their* lives. Many of us are dealing with generational curses that came down through the family line of our mother or our father. God is saying in this scripture that we can pass those same curses on down to *our* children if we choose to ignore His principles and forget His laws.

Certainly this is true in the area of finances. For instance, if Christians ignore God's principle of sowing and reaping, they will fail to receive a harvest of prosperity for themselves or their families. Many Christians who continually ignore this biblical principle in their everyday lives still go around saying, "God is my Father." But God is asking those people, "If I am your Father, where is your honor toward Me and My Word?"

Here are two undeniable scriptures that reveal how important this concept of honor is to God:

> **"A son honors his father, and a servant his master. If then I am the Father, where is My honor? And if I am a Master, where is My reverence? says the Lord of hosts to you priests who despise My name...."**

> **Malachi 1:6**

> Honor the Lord with your wealth, with the firstfruits of all your crops;
> then your barns will be filled to overflowing, and your vats will brim over with new wine.

> **Proverbs 3:9,10 *NIV***

Diligent To Do

That's why it will take a deliberate decision on your part if you are going to change your future and achieve excellence in the realm of your finances. You have to determine that you're going to help your faith continually grow by hearing and hearing and hearing the Word (Rom. 10:17).

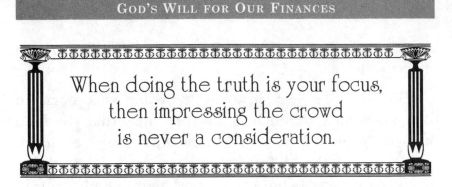

When doing the truth is your focus,
then impressing the crowd
is never a consideration.

We won't get anywhere in life by trying to live by faith according to what we *used* to hear. Faith comes as we hear the Word on a continuing basis every day of our lives. I'm not talking about gaining Bible knowledge for the sake of gaining knowledge. This is what we have to ask ourselves:

1. *Have I acted in faith on the Bible knowledge I've gained?*

2. *Am I doing what God requires of me to change my economic future?*

You see, God always has a system of checks to make sure we are who we say we are to Him. He doesn't care for lip service.

> **These people draw near to Me with their mouth, and honor Me with their lips, but their heart is far from Me.**
>
> **Matthew 15:8**

Just consider the example of Zacchaeus the tax collector (Luke 19:2-10). The crowd was grumbling about Jesus' decision to visit the home of Zacchaeus, a sinner. Everyone hated Zacchaeus. In the eyes of others, he probably squeezed people a little too hard at times. It may have even looked as if he extorted people in his position as tax collector.

But one day an intense knowing was born in Zacchaeus' heart. Suddenly he just knew that the Man named Jesus — the Teacher he had heard so much about — was the Messiah. So when Jesus came to his town, Zacchaeus (who was a short man) climbed up in a tree so he could see Him better. As Jesus walked by, He sensed virtue being pulled from Him by someone's faith and looked up.

Seeing Zacchaeus sitting there in a tree, Jesus called out, "Zacchaeus, come down, for I must go to your house and have dinner today."

Immediately the religious people started complaining to Jesus. They said, "Listen, Master, don't You know who this guy is? He's a big failure and a real crook!"

Zacchaeus could hear what the people were saying, so he turned around and said to Jesus, **"...Look, Lord, I give half of my goods to the poor; and if I have taken anything from anyone by false accusation, I restore fourfold"** (v. 8).

Zacchaeus didn't have to say anything else. He had just demonstrated his faith in Jesus with his actions. As a result, Jesus told him, **"...Today salvation has come to this house..."** (v. 9).

I am weary of the fact that so many Christians listen, listen, listen but never *do*. There is only one reason I record one more tape or write one more book: So people can take the principles I teach and *make them live again.*

If we want salvation and all that it encompasses — deliverance, wholeness, preservation, protection, healing, and abundance — to come to *our* house, there has to be enough evidence in our lives to show that we are believers. We don't have to convince anyone of anything. We don't have to impress people with our faith. We just need to *do*. As we work on impressing God by following His principles, we'll pass right by the people who blow sunshine with their words but never act on what they know.

Personally, I don't wait for someone else to tell me whether or not they see enough evidence in me to convict me of being a believer. I continually examine my life and ask *myself* that question. That's why people can look at my life and say, "You know, I may not understand that man, but I have to admit — he lives what he believes!"

If You Had More, Would You Give More?

Over the years, I've made it a point to learn how to live what I believe in the area of giving and finances. One thing I had to do was stop saying, "Lord, I'd love to give more into the Gospel, but I can't. If I only had more, I'd give more."

I realized I was just lying to myself when I said that. If I kept waiting until I had more money before I began to live the life of a giver, I'd never get started. So I decided to stop wishing I had more and just start pursuing excellence in giving with all my heart. As I did that, God's principles of increase and prosperity began to work mightily in my life.

A person who doesn't give into the Gospel when he doesn't have much money will not start giving if he ever has more. He may pray, "Lord, just give me some money so I can be a giver." He may even pray, "Lord, give me a million dollars, and I promise I'll give You half of it."

But God isn't stupid. He knows that if that person had the money, he wouldn't give it. The Bible says a person who is unfaithful with little will also be unfaithful with much. On the other hand, a person who is faithful with the little he has will still be faithful when he gains more (Luke 16:10).

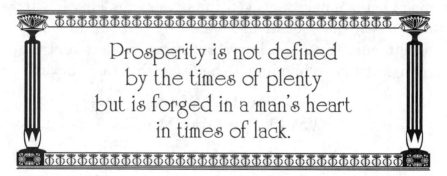

Prosperity is not defined
by the times of plenty
but is forged in a man's heart
in times of lack.

The greatest test we will ever face in our lives is not heart trouble or a brain tumor; it is the test of *prosperity*.

This is the test too many Christians fail and then never recover from. Every time they hear a message on giving, they say, "No, I don't think so. Tomorrow I'll come back and hear more about this. Maybe then I'll do something about it." But because they only *hear* the Word but never *do* what it says in the area of finances, they miss out on the blessings of abundance God has planned for them.

So what is God's will concerning our finances? He wants us to enjoy prosperity and abundance. He wants us to have more than enough to meet every need as we freely share with others.

However, we can only experience God's will in this area of our lives as we follow His principles. Otherwise, we'll just remain at the same level year after year — always claiming, "I know God has a future for me," but never seeing any increase in our lives. We'll find ourselves in the same situation as the woman with the issue of blood, who "**...spent all that she had and was no better, but rather grew worse**" (Mark 5:26). And just like this woman, our situation will only change the day we determine to pursue Jesus with all our strength.

What do *you* believe? Does God has a good future for you? Is it His will to prosper you and to give you renewed hope? Rest assured, the answer to both questions is emphatically *yes*. But allow this truth to sink deep in your heart: *There is only one way to attain God's future for you, and that is by the power of the seed.*

PRINCIPLES CONCERNING
GOD'S WILL FOR OUR FINANCES

* Influence will never be granted to us unless favor can be seen upon us.

* Heaven's clothing is never woven with the cursed patches of poverty.

* Heaven expects us to produce enough money to provide for the needs of our household.

* Heaven's will for us is to possess enough money to preach the Gospel around the world.

* Heaven demands that we have enough money to pay the tax man.

* Heaven focuses on the poor and requires us to have enough money to take care of them.

* Heaven's requirements never precede Heaven's provisions.

* Obedience and servanthood are the prerequisites for being trusted with God's prosperity.

* When doing the truth is your focus, then impressing the crowd is never a consideration.

* Prosperity is not defined by the times of plenty but is forged in a man's heart in times of lack.

★ ★ ★ ★ ★

THE POWER OF THE SEED

Why is giving so important to God? Because giving is a seed, and everything good you will ever want to attain in this life requires seed. It's a universal law, spoken forth by God in Genesis 8:22:

"While the earth remains, seedtime and harvest, cold and heat, winter and summer, and day and night shall not cease."

You may not have realized this, but in a very real sense, God is retired. After He created the earth and set His universal laws into motion, the Bible says He rested from His work (Gen. 2:2).

Meanwhile, the law of sowing and reaping that He instituted will last until the end of time. As long as the earth remains, there will be summer and winter, seedtime and harvest.

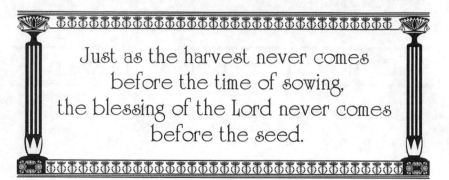

> Just as the harvest never comes
> before the time of sowing,
> the blessing of the Lord never comes
> before the seed.

We don't have to beg God or constantly cry out to Him in desperation to help us. We can actually create our own future by sowing seed.

Now, it's important to realize that the harvest hardly ever comes overnight. We may sow seed our entire lives and never see the full harvest to the seed we have sown. But let me tell you who *will* see that harvest: *our children.*

That's why we should always be asking ourselves: What is the spiritual inheritance we are leaving our children? What type of crops have we sown in our own lives that will reap a harvest in their lives? Have we sown good seed that will reap a harvest of blessing and righteousness, or bad seed that opens the door to the enemy in the years to come?

I know what I'm talking about from personal experience. I've had to buckle up, put on my helmet and harness, and pursue a higher level in life with every ounce of inner strength I could muster because of the turbulence my parents left me as an inheritance. (Before they were born again, my parents were both alcoholics. As you might imagine, much bad seed was sown as I was growing up!)

But this same principle works on the positive side as well. As we sow good seed of godly character and obedience to the Lord before our children, we can rest assured that a harvest of God's blessings will come into their lives as our reward. We can count on that harvest as an established fact, because God said so in His Word. As long as this earth remains, seedtime and harvest will not cease.

Although this issue of sowing good seed for our future applies to every area of our lives, in this discussion we'll focus on the realm of finances. I want to share with you what it means to pursue excellence in giving through the power of the seed.

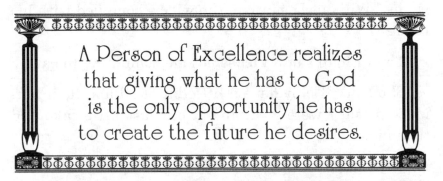

A Person of Excellence realizes
that giving what he has to God
is the only opportunity he has
to create the future he desires.

First Kings 17 talks about a woman who literally saved not only her own life but the life of her son because she followed this principle. We know her as the widow of Zarephath.

The widow of Zarephath was living in the midst of a long famine and was on her last little bit of oil and meal. But because this woman had faith, God moved on her behalf. In fact, the Lord actually dried up the brook Cherith where Elijah had been staying so that the prophet could respond to the faith of this woman.

This is an example of something you can count on as you pursue a life of excellence in God:

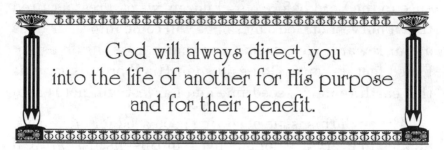

God will always direct you into the life of another for His purpose and for their benefit.

When Elijah arrived at the city gates of Zarephath, he saw the widow out there, gathering up sticks to cook her last meager supper. Elijah said, "Please bring me some water." Without hesitation, the widow complied with his request.

Then Elijah said, "Please get me something to eat."

She said, "I only have a little bit of oil and flour left. My son and I were going to eat our last little cake and then die."

Elijah replied, "Don't be afraid; it isn't going to happen like that. Just make a little cake for me first and then for you and your son."

I can see the "Zarephath Times" headlines now: "MAN OF GOD TAKES THE LAST LITTLE CAKE FROM A WIDOW WOMAN!" Elijah's request just doesn't make sense to man's natural reasoning. Nevertheless, the widow woman stepped out in faith and obeyed Elijah's instructions.

Notice that the Bible doesn't even say the woman obeyed *the Word of God*. Rather, it says she obeyed *the word of Elijah.* You see, she was spiritually activating the power of the seed by following this scriptural principle: *Giving what you have to God is the only chance you have to create the future you desire.*

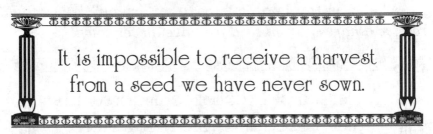

It is impossible to receive a harvest from a seed we have never sown.

Why do so many Christians believe they can receive something from someone that they are not willing to give themselves? It doesn't work that way in God's Kingdom. A person cannot receive what he isn't willing to give.

Always keep this in mind: *Anything you refuse to sow is something you consider to be more valuable than the harvest you could potentially reap.*

People sometimes say to me, "I've been believing God for a million dollars."

When I hear that, I think to myself, *But would you be willing to give a million dollars if you had it? If not, you'll still be believing for a million dollars when you die.*

I have a friend who tells the story of the time he moved into his new building and said to the Lord, "Lord, I want to give away my old building. It's worth almost a half a million dollars, so just tell me what Christian ministry I should give this building to."

Then the Lord spoke to his heart and said, "Son, quit praying about that."

"Why, Lord?" he asked.

"Because no ministry has even sown the kind of seed that would reap a harvest like this building."

What was the Lord saying to my friend? *We cannot receive a harvest from seed we have never sown.*

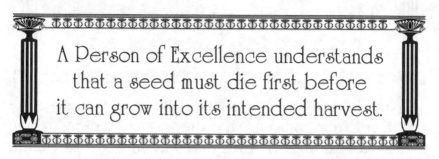

A Person of Excellence understands that a seed must die first before it can grow into its intended harvest.

It's also important to remember that when you sow your seed, it must die first in order for it to take root and begin to grow. This is the stage called "the loss of vision."

However, although your vision may seem dormant for a while, rest assured that the seed is taking root. In the foundational part of life where progress can't always be seen, God is working to bring the vision to pass. As you hold fast to your faith in the coming harvest, your God-given vision will spring up and live again, causing your joy to be made full.

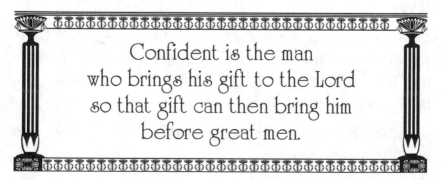

Confident is the man who brings his gift to the Lord so that gift can then bring him before great men.

.   Proverbs 18:16 says, **"A man's gift makes room for him and brings him before great men."** Now, Christians often have the idea that this verse is talking about a person's talents, such as the ability to sing well or skillfully counsel others. But that isn't what this verse is talking about here. He's talking about the giving of substance. A man's gift of substance will make room for him and will bring him before great men.

The *New Living Translation* says it this way: **"Giving a gift works wonders; it may bring you before important people!"** Why does giving a gift work wonders? *Because whatever anointing you respect, you will attract.*

How can I tell a person that I care for him without showing him through giving? I can't. And I can't give to him just one time and stop, because excellence is an everyday pursuit. Excellence doesn't know a day when it can say, "I quit. I've gotten what I wanted, so I'm no longer going to give." No, excellence is always in for the long haul. If it isn't committed for the long haul, it isn't excellence.

Proverbs 17:8 also talks about the importance of a gift: **"A present is a precious stone in the eyes of its possessor; wherever he turns, he prospers."** Then in Proverbs 21:14 (*KJV*), we see that God also uses gifts to settle arguments: **"A gift in secret pacifieth anger: and a reward in the bosom strong wrath."**

This principle was in operation when God ended the argument between Himself and mankind by sending Jesus: **"For God so loved the world that He gave His only begotten Son..."** (John 3:16). When Jesus died on that Cross, that was it — the argument was over. God said, "Okay, I have paid the ransom. Jesus has paid the price for all mankind. They're all Mine now. I'm getting them back from the hands of the enemy."

So many people — including many Christians — don't understand the importance and power of giving and are therefore trapped by their own genetics and cultural backgrounds. Some people even live and die within two blocks of where they were born because their socioeconomic background has held them prisoner. They're stuck in an invisible box created both by genetics and environment, and they have no idea how to get out of that box.

I was once in that position, but I was determined to find out how to get out of that box. I went to the Word to discover what I needed to do to leave behind the socioeconomic rat race in which I'd never do anything but continue to produce what my parents and grandparents produced during their lifetimes. I wanted to know what God said I needed to change in my life in order to transform my socioeconomic level.

Understand this: The strongholds, sins, bad habits, and negative ways of thinking that we are dealing with in our lives right now are nothing more than the harvest of the four generations that came before us — our parents, our grandparents, our great-grandparents, and our great-great-grandparents. That can drive us up a wall, especially when we don't even know what we're dealing with.

But I found out that our lives don't have to be defined by the sins of both family lines for the past four hundred years. Once I understood this truth, I stopped reacting when something negative showed up in my life. I quit thinking, *Oh, rats, what did I do that for? I should have never done that. That was horrible.*

I don't think that way anymore. When I see something negative in my life, I deal with it according to the Word. But I don't waste time blaming myself. I don't jump up and down in frustration or find a place to hide in condemnation. I just recognize that I have once more experienced a demonstration of my personal genetic code.

I'm telling you, we have to break the power of yesterday in our lives! If we don't, we'll continually crash in situation after situation; then we'll wonder why God didn't bring us through in victory: *God, why didn't You come through for me? What's wrong with me? Why can't I succeed?*

We never have to go through that mess. God has given us principles by which we can change our future. And in this area of giving and finances, one principle stands out from all others: *the power of the seed.* This is the key that will release us from the socioeconomic box that has trapped us for so long. This is the divine catalyst that will bring us before great men.

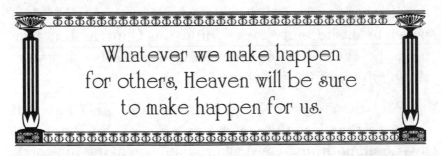

Whatever we make happen
for others, Heaven will be sure
to make happen for us.

People in the world have a million reasons why they pursue a career or go to work every day. For instance, they might want to raise their standard of living or gain status in the eyes of others.

But what is *God's* will for the workplace? According to His perspective, what is the primary reason we are to go to work each day?

To answer that question, let's look first at First Corinthians 12:31 (*AMP*):

> **But earnestly desire and zealously cultivate the greatest and best gifts and graces (the higher gifts and the choicest graces). And yet I will show you a still more excellent way [one that is better by far and the highest of them all — love].**

Paul goes on to talk about the paramount importance of love:

> **Though I speak with the tongues of men and of angels, but have not love** [if love is not the reason I'm doing what I'm doing], **I have become sounding brass or a clanging cymbal.**

> **1 Corinthians 13:1**

In essence Paul is saying, "I may operate mightily in spiritual gifts, including the gift of tongues God has given to me to edify myself and the Church. But love must be the basis for exercising them all; otherwise, these gifts profit me nothing."

Paul then says in verse 2, "**...And though I have all faith, so that I could remove mountains, but have not love, I am nothing.**" Once again, Paul is making the point, "Even if my faith gave me the ability to cast mountains into the sea, I would still be nothing if love wasn't the reason I was doing it." Now look at verse 3:

And though I bestow all my goods to feed the poor, and though I give my body to be burned, but have not love, it profits me nothing.

Paul is talking about giving, about taking care of the poor, even about martyrdom — all of which are good deeds that men praise. But again Paul says, "If love is not the motivation that causes me to do what I'm doing, it profits me nothing."

God's message is clear: We are not to do *anything* in self-centeredness. Our entire lives are to be spent in service for others, not for ourselves. "If love isn't the reason I'm doing good works," Paul says, "I am wasting my time — even if I lay down my life in a martyr's death."

So many times people only do things for themselves. Proverbs 16:26 says it like this:

The person who labors, labors for himself, for his hungry mouth drives him on.

Why do people go to work? Because they're hungry. But that's not the reason Christians are to go to work. They are to work for the reason set forth in Ephesians 4:28:

Let him who stole steal no longer, but rather let him labor, working with his hands what is good, that he may have something to give him who has need.

In other words, you don't go to work for yourself; you go to work for the person next to you.

That's why you never have to get upset about your job or despise what you do in the workplace. After all, when you go to work, you're going there for someone else. You can therefore go through your workday, confident that Jesus will meet your needs as you labor to meet someone else's needs through your sowing.

God has assigned someone to give to you in order to meet your needs. Why? Because you're not going to work so you can buy a better house or a better car — you're going to work so that another man can live. Of course, God wants to give you a car, and He wants to put money in your bank account. But He *doesn't* want *you* to labor in your own strength to do it all by yourself.

Always keep this in mind: Money that comes through our hands might actually be someone else's money — and the day we put our hands to someone else's money is the day we become thieves. I guarantee you, that is the day we can't afford!

Therefore, consider the money you earn at your job as a potential blessing for someone else, just waiting for an assignment. As you seek the Lord for guidance, He will show you how much to spend on your own needs and what is to be sown into good ground for a later harvest.

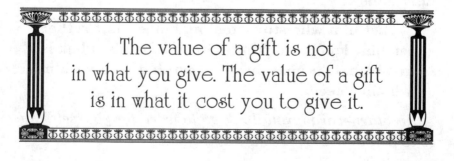

The value of a gift is not
in what you give. The value of a gift
is in what it cost you to give it.

A person of excellence is always a person of manners. He never takes anything for granted in the life of another — *never*. Everything is a gift, a privilege, for which he is continually thankful.

Personally, I make sure I never take anything or anyone for granted. I don't take a gift for granted, no matter how small it is. If someone comes to me and hands me a dollar, I'm thankful for the seed that person has sown.

Now, to someone else the gift of a dollar may seem very insignificant, but not to me. In fact, that dollar is as significant as a thousand or ten thousand dollars is to me. Why is this? First, that person is activating the power of the seed by sowing into my life. Second, it's possible that he has given all he has to give when he hands me that dollar.

This was the situation when the widow woman gave her offering in Mark 12:41-44:

> Now Jesus sat opposite the treasury and saw how the people put money into the treasury. And many who were rich put in much.
>
> Then one poor widow came and threw in two mites, which make a quadrans.
>
> So He called His disciples to Himself and said to them, "Assuredly, I say to you that this poor widow has put in more than all those who have given to the treasury;
>
> "for they all put in out of their abundance, but she out of her poverty put in all that she had, her whole livelihood."

The widow woman came in the temple with everyone else to give her offering. Inside the temple court were metal offering containers. As the people put in their offerings, the constant noise of coins hitting metal filled the crowded room.

But people always knew when a wealthy person put in his large offering, because the large number of coins hitting the metal container would make a huge noise. Everyone would turn around to see who had given such an impressive offering, which is exactly what the wealthy person wanted.

Meanwhile, Jesus was standing nearby, watching the people put their offerings into the temple treasury. He saw the rich religious rulers dump in their large offerings, but Jesus wasn't fooled. He knew the hidden desire for recognition that motivated their generous giving.

Then this widow woman came shuffling up to the offering container and put in two mites — worth about a half-penny. With all the noise from the other people's larger offerings, Jesus couldn't even hear the widow's coins as she threw them in. Nevertheless, this little woman's offering got Jesus excited.

"*Wow!* Did you see *that*?" Jesus asked His disciples.

The disciples started looking around, saying, "What? Where? Who? Who did what?"

They didn't recognize what had just happened, but Jesus saw something very significant in the widow woman's tiny offering.

Someone might say, "I know what this scripture proves — that Jesus loves poverty."

No, that isn't it at all. When that woman came into the temple and put in those two mites, in God's eyes she put in more than all the others. Why? *Because the value of a gift is not in what a person gives. Its value is in what it cost that person to give it.* The widow put in more than all the others because she gave all that she had.

Too many times people are happy to give something that doesn't cost them anything. But I won't do that. I will not offer to God something that costs me nothing. I know I am not to just give out of my substance carelessly. I must be hooked up in faith to my giving on the inside.

That's why David said, "I will never give anything to the Lord that costs me nothing" (2 Sam. 24:24). At that moment, David was in trouble with the Lord because he had taken a census of the children of Israel. Perhaps it was pride that motivated David to take the census. All we know is that something about that one act opened the door for a plague to spread throughout the land.

Look at the Bible's account of how David stopped the plague:

> **Now Araunah looked, and saw the king and his servants coming toward him. So Araunah went out and bowed before the king with his face to the ground.**
>
> **Then Araunah said, "Why has my lord the king come to his servant?" And David said, "To buy the threshing floor from you, to build an altar to**

the Lord, that the plague may be withdrawn from the people."

Now Araunah said to David, "Let my lord the king take and offer up whatever seems good to him. Look, here are oxen for burnt sacrifice, and threshing implements and the yokes of the oxen for wood.

"All these, O king, Araunah has given to the king." And Araunah said to the king, "May the Lord your God accept you."

Then the king said to Araunah, "No, but I will surely buy it from you for a price; nor will I offer burnt offerings to the Lord my God with that which costs me nothing." So David bought the threshing floor and the oxen for fifty shekels of silver.

And David built there an altar to the Lord, and offered burnt offerings and peace offerings. So the Lord heeded the prayers for the land, and the plague was withdrawn from Israel.

2 Samuel 24:20-25

David understood this important truth: If a gift doesn't cost us something, it is insignificant in our eyes, no matter how large it seems. And if the seed we sow is insignificant to us, it is also insignificant to God.

That's one reason many people don't receive any fruit from the seed they sow — because they're constantly giving God that which costs them nothing. People who do that are making no room for God to bless them.

That's why I have become a compulsive giver of gifts that cost me something. I am an incurable seed-sower, and I don't want to be cured. I have to show love to everyone around me. I will leave nothing unloved or untouched by my giving, for I know that everything in life that we love, we must give to.

If your gift costs you little to give it, it is of little benefit to your life. Therefore, I urge you to make the same decision David did: "I will not give anything to the Lord that costs me nothing."

I'm talking about tapping into the power of the seed in your life. No principle I could ever share with you is as vital to attaining excellence in the realm of finances. It's a key that will unlock untold doors of opportunity, leading straight into a bright and glorious future in God!

PRINCIPLES FOR
THE POWER OF THE SEED

★ Just as the harvest never comes before the time of sowing, the blessing of the Lord never comes before the seed.

★ A Person of Excellence realizes that giving what he has to God is the only opportunity he has to create the future he desires.

★ God will always direct you into the life of another for His purpose and for their benefit.

★ It is impossible to receive a harvest from a seed we have never sown.

★ A Person of Excellence understands that a seed must die first before it can grow into its intended harvest.

★ Confident is the man who brings his gift to the Lord so that gift can then bring him before great men.

★ Whatever we make happen for others, Heaven will be sure to make happen for us.

★ The value of a gift is not in what you give. The value of a gift is in what it cost you to give it.

NOTES:

CHAPTER THREE

$$\bigstar \bigstar \bigstar \bigstar \bigstar$$

YOUR GIVING DETERMINES YOUR FUTURE

Once you've grasped this concept of the power of the seed, your next thought might be, *But I just don't have any seed to sow right now.*

I remember when I was in that exact situation as a new Christian. I was sitting in a meeting, and I literally didn't have one penny to give. But I wanted to give *something*, so I broke a pencil in half and put the eraser end of the pencil in the offering envelope. Then with the other half of the pencil, I wrote my name on the envelope and dropped it in the offering bucket!

That's where my life of giving started. Until that moment, my past history had left me with nothing but pain. But from that day forward, my life began an upward ascent that has never stopped.

The power of the seed changed my life drastically for the better, and it will do the same for you. I want to share some principles along this line that you can apply to your life for a better future. We'll also look at some biblical examples of people who created an entirely new future for themselves through a quality decision to give from the heart.

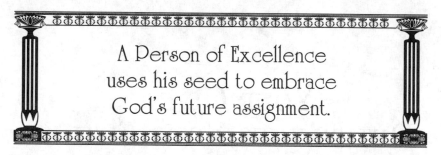

A Person of Excellence uses his seed to embrace God's future assignment.

Solomon understood this principle. We see in Second Chronicles 1 that he used the power of the seed to create a future for himself.

> **And Solomon went up there to the bronze altar before the Lord, which was at the tabernacle of meeting, and offered a thousand burnt offerings on it.**
> **On that night God appeared to Solomon, and said to him, "Ask! What shall I give you?"**
>
> 2 Chronicles 1:6,7

Before Solomon went up to that bronze altar, he had a problem. He had to find a way to fill the shoes of his father David, the pastor of Israel. But how could Solomon follow the footsteps of greatness? After all, it was King David who had turned Israel back to God through his own intimate, living relationship with the Lord.

The thought of following in his father's footsteps must have made Solomon shake in his boots. The young man probably lay awake nights, wondering if the people would constantly compare him to his father and possibly even reject him as king. How could he ever measure up to the legacy David had left him to live up to?

Then came the day Solomon went to the tabernacle and offered one thousand burnt offerings to the Lord. That very same night, God appeared to him and asked, "What can I do for you?"

Think about that. Here was a man who had just been given the job of governing the greatest kingdom on the face of the earth. But as a servant of the true and the living God, Solomon realized he needed to plant seed in the ground in order to bring forth the harvest of provision required to fulfill that great responsibility.

So make no mistake about it — Solomon offered those sacrifices to the Lord on purpose. He wanted to get God's attention, and he did! Just try to imagine the scene as one thousand animals were offered in a single day. Solomon and the Levites who prepared the animal sacrifices must have been ankle deep in blood!

Solomon definitely got God's attention through his giving that day. The power of that seed produced results before even one day had passed!

So what was Solomon's response when God appeared to him that night and asked, "What can I do for you?" Well, one thing Solomon *didn't* say was, "Gosh, I haven't been thinking about that, Lord. Give me some time to come up with an answer." No, Solomon knew what he wanted to say to the Lord:

And Solomon said to God: "You have shown great mercy to David my father, and have made me king in his place.

"Now, O Lord God, let Your promise to David my father be established, for You have made me king over a people like the dust of the earth in multitude.

"Now give me wisdom and knowledge, that I may go out and come in before this people; for who can judge this great people of Yours?"

2 Chronicles 1:8-10

Solomon had obviously been considering his answer long before the moment he was asked the question. He knew God was coming. No one had ever sown the way he had that day.

Solomon had deliberately acted on this principle of prosperity; then he waited for the expected outcome.

> A Person of Excellence understands that in order to obtain something he has never had, he has to do something he has never done.

God liked Solomon's humble answer. Verses 11 and 12 give the Lord's response:

Then God said to Solomon: "Because this was in your heart, and you have not asked riches or

wealth or honor or the life of your enemies, nor have you asked long life — but have asked wisdom and knowledge for yourself, that you may judge My people over whom I have made you king —

"wisdom and knowledge are granted to you; and I will give you riches and wealth and honor, such as none of the kings have had who were before you, nor shall any after you have the like."

Here's something important we can learn from Solomon in this passage of Scripture: *We have to use wisdom in what we ask God for.* For instance, if we pray, "Lord, make me more of a giver," that request already takes into account our need to have more money. So we don't have to ask God for money; we just need to ask Him for help in becoming better givers.

Solomon understood what to ask God for. The young king knew that in order to be a wise judge before his people, God would have to help him remain dominant over his enemies. Why? Because God doesn't get at all excited about His people getting killed all the time. His heart is to preserve His people from harm. But in order to fulfill that desire, God needed a wise leader for His people — someone who could adequately follow a tough act like David.

So Solomon asked for wisdom and received much more. He didn't ask for money, but he received riches and wealth and honor above all the kings before and after him.

Solomon grasped a truth that we all need to understand:

The Excellent are aware that
the laws of God are to be obeyed —
not discussed.

Far too many Christians are walking around saying, "I'm the head and not the tail," but their tails are dragging behind them everywhere they go! But if a person is the head on the inside, he needs to be the head on the outside as well. Otherwise, all he's doing is peddling hope to a lost world.

So it was through Solomon's giving that he was able to embrace God's assignment for his future. Don't hesitate to follow Solomon's example. You get God's attention when you plant seed in the ground in anticipation of *your* future harvest!

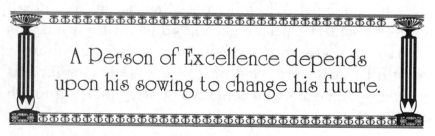

A Person of Excellence depends
upon his sowing to change his future.

First Kings 10 relates an important event that happened later as a manifestation of God's promise to Solomon that night — a visit from the Queen of Sheba. At the time of this historic visit, Solomon's fame had already spread throughout the known world. The queen came to find out for herself if his reputation for wisdom and wealth was truly justified.

As a result of that visit, Solomon experienced an even greater increase in wealth and in his stature as king. But it's important to remember as you read this account that the Queen of Sheba came only *after* Solomon sowed seed — in this case, one thousand burnt offerings before the Lord.

> **Now when the queen of Sheba heard of the fame of Solomon concerning the name of the Lord, she came to test him with hard questions.**
>
> **She came to Jerusalem with a very great retinue, with camels that bore spices, very much gold, and precious stones; and when she came to Solomon, she spoke with him about all that was in her heart.**
>
> **So Solomon answered all her questions; there was nothing so difficult for the king that he could not explain it to her.**
>
> **1 Kings 10:1-3**

The queen traveled about 1,300 miles by camel to see this king whose wisdom she had heard so much about. Compare this woman's desire for wisdom to most people in our modern-day society. Preachers have a hard time convincing people to travel thirteen miles to church in a car, much less 1300 miles on a camel! The difference in response lies in the value that is placed on the gift. What a person considers common will only provide him with a common benefit.

The queen didn't travel those 1,300 miles to Solomon's court alone. A huge retinue of servants and livestock accompanied her, carrying enormous amounts of spices, gold, and other precious goods that she planned to give to the king if he proved himself worthy. I'm sure a small army also accompanied the queen to protect all the valuables she brought with her.

On the day the queen arrived at the palace, King Solomon probably asked his chamberlain, "Who is on the docket for today?"

"Well, there is the customary long line of people waiting to come in one at a time to speak with you and hear your wisdom."

"Who is that woman with all the servants and camels at the back of the line?"

"That's the Queen of Sheba. Those camels are carrying all the gifts she brought for you."

"Well, bring her to the front of the line!"

(How can I know that it probably happened this way? Because I believe the Bible, which says in Proverbs 19:6, **"Many entreat the favor of the nobility, and every man is a friend to one who gives gifts."**)

But why had the Queen of Sheba come to Solomon's court bearing so many gifts? Because she was a person of excellence in her own right, and she grasped the importance of understanding wisdom.

According to Proverbs 4:7, this is a truth we all need to get ahold of: **"Wisdom is the principal thing; therefore get wisdom. And in all your getting, get understanding."** In other words, we have to get interested not only in *hearing* wisdom, but in *understanding* wisdom. We are not to live our lives as those who just know wisdom principles but never live what they know.

The Queen of Sheba was thirsting for wisdom. She came to King Solomon's court because she had heard about his great wisdom and the splendor of his court. Now she wanted to see for herself if all the things she had heard about Solomon were true.

First Kings 10:4-9 tells us the queen's response to all she observed during her visit to the land of Israel:

> **And when the queen of Sheba had seen all the wisdom of Solomon, the house that he had built, the food on his table, the seating of his servants, the service of his waiters and their apparel, his cupbearers, and his entryway by which he went up to the house of the Lord, there was no more spirit in her.**
>
> **Then she said to the king: "It was a true report which I heard in my own land about your words and your wisdom.**
>
> **"However I did not believe the words until I came and saw with my own eyes; and indeed the half was not told me. Your wisdom and prosperity exceed the fame of which I heard."**
>
> **"Happy are your men and happy are these your servants, who stand continually before you and hear your wisdom!**
>
> **"Blessed be the Lord your God, who delighted in you, setting you on the throne of Israel! Because the Lord has loved Israel forever, therefore He made you king, to do justice and righteousness."**

What the queen saw during her visit to Solomon's court far exceeded what she had heard about him. She saw more than what other people had told her about the young king because she could recognize things other people couldn't recognize. She *heard* a demonstration of Solomon's great wisdom when he responded to her hard questions. She also *saw* a demonstration of his wisdom as she observed the way he ascended unto the house of the Lord, not to mention the magnificent house he had built, the rich food on his table, and the excellent way his servants dressed and conducted themselves as they served the guests.

You see, wisdom can be seen, not just heard. Jesus said concerning wisdom, **"...Wisdom is proved right by her actions"** (Matt. 11:19 *NIV*). In other words, wisdom is always justified by its product, not by its voice.

If you want to know whether or not a person is truly wise, look at his life rather than what he says. Don't waste your time with people who just want to talk and never put action to their words. Focus on building relationships with productive people who are continually moving toward excellence in every area of their lives, including the area of finances.

In Solomon's case, the queen saw evidence of his wisdom in his *prosperity*. Remember, she said she came to Solomon's court not believing what she had heard. That means she probably withheld who she was from Solomon as she took the time to observe the way he ruled his kingdom.

But by the end of her visit, all traces of pride and reserve had disappeared from the Queen of Sheba. The sum total of all that she experienced in Solomon's court was more than she could comprehend. It took her breath away and left her awestruck as she exclaimed, **"...Indeed the half was not told me. Your wisdom and prosperity exceed the fame of which I heard"** (v. 7).

Do you know what keeps a person from being able to receive excellence from others? Pride. Whenever someone competes with excellence, he becomes disqualified from receiving the benefits of that excellence. You see, excellence in someone's life is always a reward, not something to be competed against.

The Queen of Sheba grasped that truth and responded with joy to the excellence she observed in the life and kingdom of Solomon. And what was the queen's next response to Solomon's excellence? *She gave.*

> **Then she gave the king one hundred and twenty talents of gold, spices in great quantity, and precious stones. There never again came such abundance of spices as the queen of Sheba gave to King Solomon.**
>
> **1 Kings 10:10**

Let me share the principle that applies here:

The Excellent realize that
reward will never be experienced
in their lives until someone
first recognizes their excellence.

Too many Christians try to "shake God down" for money by crying and begging Him for it. These are often the same people who live from miracle to miracle as they face one financial crisis after the other.

But God never wanted us to live *from miracle to miracle*. He wants us to live *from glory to glory*. This level in life can only be attained, however, as a result of pursuing excellence that others can recognize and thus desire to reward.

Despite all the gifts that the Queen of Sheba lavished on King Solomon, she left his presence with far more than she had given. In Matthew 12:42, Jesus gave us a clue regarding what the queen received during that visit:

"The queen of the South will rise up in the judgment with this generation and condemn it, for she came from the ends of the earth to hear the wisdom of Solomon; and indeed a greater than Solomon is here."

In other words, when the queen went to see Solomon, she didn't just *hear* his wisdom. She *received* that wisdom in her heart so that by the time she left Solomon's court, she was a believer in the God of Israel! That's why she will be a witness against the Jewish religious leaders — because she received the truth that they ultimately rejected.

I'm sure the Queen of Sheba's life was never the same after that visit. But what was it that changed her future? *Her giving.* And it is *your* giving that will change your future as well.

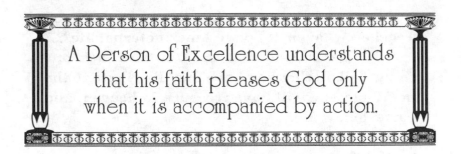

A Person of Excellence understands
that his faith pleases God only
when it is accompanied by action.

Hebrews 11:6 says that without faith, it is impossible to please God. But that verse isn't talking about the kind of faith that hears the Word without ever doing anything about it. The only faith that pleases God is the kind that has actions to go along with it. And since our giving determines our future, this principle is especially relevant in the area of finances.

Let me share some biblical examples of people who acted on their faith by giving and thus changed their futures forever. First, let's look at what Zacchaeus did when he placed his faith in Jesus as the Messiah. As we saw earlier, Zacchaeus' faith was immediately followed by action when he said, **"...Look, Lord, I give half of my goods to the poor; and if I have taken anything from anyone by false accusation, I restore fourfold"** (Luke 19:8).

Jesus' response revealed His pleasure with Zacchaeus' act of faith: **"...Today salvation has come to this house..."** (v. 9).

In contrast, the rich ruler in Luke 18 did *not* act in faith when he heard Jesus' instructions to give:

> Now a certain ruler asked Him, saying, "Good Teacher, what shall I do to inherit eternal life?..."
>
> ...He [Jesus] said to him, "You still lack one thing. Sell all that you have and distribute to the poor, and you will have treasure in heaven; and come, follow Me."
>
> But when he heard this, he became very sorrowful, for he was very rich.
>
> Luke 18:18,22,23

The ruler wasn't willing to act in faith on Jesus' words. He started thinking about all the material possessions he had. (In reality, all those material possessions had *him*!) In the end, he turned around and sadly walked away.

Whereas Zacchaeus wanted Jesus more than he wanted riches, this ruler wanted the riches more than he wanted Jesus. Rather than choosing to sow for his future, the ruler chose to keep what he had in his present. Consequently, this man lost the opportunity to change his future by the power of the seed.

So of these two men — Zacchaeus and the rich ruler — who do you think came out on top in the end, both in the natural realm and in the spiritual realm? I guarantee you that the answer is *Zacchaeus*. This principle of giving explains why:

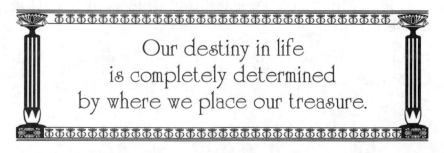

Our destiny in life
is completely determined
by where we place our treasure.

Whatever a person is willing to give up is the very thing God is willing to multiply back to him in full measure. The rich ruler put his treasure in himself and lost Heaven. But as soon as Zacchaeus heard about Jesus, he started pursuing Him.

When Zacchaeus couldn't see Jesus in the crowd, he didn't give up and go home. Instead, he climbed up in a tree. When the religious people started complaining about Jesus coming to his house, again Zacchaeus didn't give up. Instead, he exclaimed, "If I've stolen anything from anyone, I will give back to them fourfold. And half of my goods I will give to feed the poor!"

Jesus just looked at the religious Jews and asked, "What are you going to do with *that*? I tell you, salvation has come to Zacchaeus' house this day!" In other words, Zacchaeus determined the outcome of his future by where he put his treasure the day that Jesus visited his house!

You may say, "But I don't really have a good place to put my treasure."

Just ask God to show you good ground where you can start sowing some seed. God certainly didn't tell you to sow and then leave you without a field where you can put your treasure!

Now let's talk about the apostle Barnabas, who started out with the name of Joseph. We find the first mention of this man in Acts 4:36,37 (*NIV*):

> **Joseph, a Levite from Cyprus, whom the apostles called Barnabas (which means Son of Encouragement),**

sold a field he owned and brought the money and put it at the apostles' feet.

Joseph was a giver who brought refreshing and encouragement to others — so much so that they changed his name to Barnabas, or "Son of Encouragement"! (Think about it — how many people do *you* know whose names been changed because of their giving?)

This scripture says that Joseph sold some real estate that he owned and brought the proceeds to lay at the apostles' feet. Why did he do that? Because of this principle of giving:

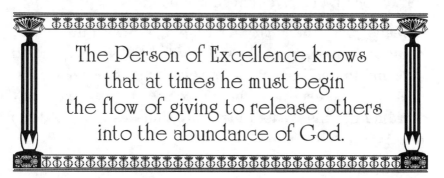

The Person of Excellence knows
that at times he must begin
the flow of giving to release others
into the abundance of God.

Sometimes when I am in a church service, God uses me to begin the flow of giving. Before I make a move, nothing is happening. Everyone is holding back his money as the minister shares the needs of a missionary in another country.

Then I lift my hand and say, "I'll take care of that need." Immediately a flood of offerings starts pouring in that is more than enough to pay for the missionary's needs. This is often what it takes to release others into abundance. Joseph, or Barnabas, understood this principle.

Later Barnabas went on to fulfill his call as an apostle, traveling throughout the land with Paul to proclaim the Gospel of Jesus Christ. Why was God was able to use Barnabas so mightily? Because Barnabas put actions behind his faith and made giving to others a lifestyle.

Acts 9:36-42 tells us about an older woman named Tabitha (surnamed Dorcas), who had also earned the reputation of a giver. She was like a church mother to the rest of the believers, a compassionate woman who loved to give to the poor and to bless people with articles of clothing that she had sewn.

But one day this kind woman fell sick and died, and her death deeply affected everyone who had known her. When her grieving friends found out that Peter was staying in nearby Joppa at the home of Simon the tanner, they sent two men to go and entreat the apostle to come back with them.

Peter hurried back with the two men. When they arrived at the house where Tabitha's body lay, the women brought out all the garments she had made to bless others. "See all Tabitha did for others, Peter," they pleaded. "Please lay your hands on her that she would live."

Peter asked everyone to leave the room. Once he was alone with Tabitha's body, he knelt down and prayed; then he simply said unto her, "Tabitha, arise." Suddenly Tabitha opened her eyes and sat up!

Tabitha's giving certainly changed *her* future, didn't it? She literally got a second chance at life when she was raised from the dead! Remember, no one had even tried to raise the dishonest Ananias from the dead (*see* Acts 5).

No one prayed for Ananias' wife Sapphira either when she fell dead at Peter's feet — and all she did was agree with a liar!

Tabitha's life reflected this principle of giving:

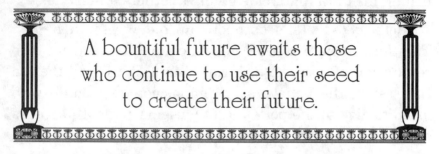

A bountiful future awaits those who continue to use their seed to create their future.

What if Tabitha had never planted any seed? There would have been no harvest for her to look forward to as she lay on her deathbed — only a cold, hard grave. But Tabitha was a person of excellence. She knew that at the moment she needed a harvest, it would come. She had sown well, and the power of that seed literally transformed her future.

Let's consider the example of the woman with the alabaster box for a moment. This was a woman who, because of her own wrong choices in life, had no real hope for the future. No one wanted to be associated with her. She probably had a few illegitimate children. The die was already cast — her life was a failure.

But one day something ignited in this woman's heart as she listened to Jesus preach His message of God's love. And when she heard that Jesus was eating dinner at Simon the leper's home, she defied all convention in order to show her love for the Master.

Walking past all the Pharisees and prominent Jews sitting at the table, the woman fell down at the feet of Jesus and began weeping. Then after wiping away her tears from His feet with her long hair, she broke open an alabaster box full of expensive spikenard — worth an entire year's wages — and anointed Him with the precious ointment.

This woman knew that once that box was open, it could never be closed again. She knew that she was giving away her most valuable possession in one act of giving. But it didn't matter to her. She was making a conscious choice to give her all — a choice born out of faith and a deep love for the Master.

With that act of extravagant giving, this woman defined her future. Some of the disciples protested that the ointment could have been sold and the money given to the poor. But Jesus brushed aside their protests, telling them, **"Assuredly, I say to you, wherever this gospel is preached in the whole world, what this woman has done will also be told as a memorial to her"** (Mark 14:9).

I want to share one more example of a person who changed his future with giving. In my view, the Roman centurion named Cornelius spoken of in Acts 10 stands out from all the rest as the perfect example of what I'm talking about.

It is possible that this centurion is also the one who asked Jesus to heal his dying servant (Luke 7:1-5). The centurion in Luke 7 actually sent the Jewish leaders to see Jesus, believing that he himself was unworthy to go to Him. The fact that the centurion was able to ask the Jewish leaders to go to Jesus on his behalf indicates that this man had a great deal of influence with the Jews. In Luke 7:4 and 5, the religious leaders explained why they held the centurion in such high esteem:

> **And when they came to Jesus, they begged Him earnestly, saying that the one for whom He should do this was deserving,**
> **"for he loves our nation, and has built us a synagogue."**

How did the Jews know that the centurion loved their people? Because he had built them a synagogue. His love for the Jewish people wasn't just a bunch of empty words; he followed up his words with action by *giving*. Only then did the centurion ask the Jewish elders to petition Jesus on behalf of his servant. The centurion was acting on this principle of giving:

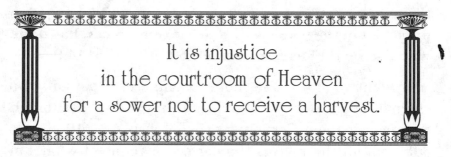

It is injustice
in the courtroom of Heaven
for a sower not to receive a harvest.

Thus, the centurion was putting a demand on his reaping when he said to the Jewish elders, "Please go tell Jesus I need Him *now*."

Now let's look at what God said to Cornelius the centurion in Acts 10. As a Gentile, Cornelius wasn't allowed to pray with the Jews. Yet verse 1 says that he didn't let that stop him from praying; he just found a place to pray alone at the Jewish hour of prayer.

As Cornelius prayed, an angel of the Lord appeared in his room and said unto him, "Cornelius."

Startled, Cornelius asked, "What is it, Lord?"

The angel replied, "Your prayers and your giving have been noticed by God" (v. 4). Then the angel went on to give Cornelius instructions that led not only to his own salvation, but that of his entire household!

God notices our giving. We may not be extremely gifted or talented, but that doesn't matter. All that matters is how much we're willing to give of ourselves and of our substance in service to Him. That's why He wants us to get our Christianity out of the realm of talent and into the realm of sowing.

I need to share an important principle right here:

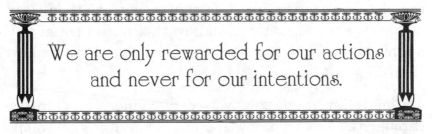

We are only rewarded for our actions and never for our intentions.

We should never expect God to reward us for our intentions when we don't follow up those intentions with *action*.

"Well, I intended to finish that task. At least give me credit for that."

But that isn't the way it works in God's Kingdom. We're not rewarded on our jobs or in our marriages because of our intentions. In the same way, we're not rewarded for merely intending to give. In every area of life — and that definitely includes our finances — God rewards us for what we actually do.

You have to understand something — the only moments that will remain of your life throughout eternity are the moments when Heaven takes a snapshot of you. What do you want Heaven's last snapshot of you to be? Personally, I want it to be a snapshot of my seed.

I want God to hear my name so much that He has to come down Himself to see what I'm giving in order to further His Kingdom on earth. I want my life to affect Jesus the way Stephen's life did — to such an extent that Jesus actually stood up to honor Stephen just before the disciple breathed his last breath.

That is my passion. Although I'm thankful to be a child of God, that isn't my final goal. I want to please God completely — one hundred percent — with no thought of "What do I get out of this?" I know that until I get myself out of the way, I'll never be able to receive God's highest according to *His* way.

I'm telling you how you can change your future through the avenue of sowing. The Scriptures give you no other way to do it. I know, because I dug into the Word to look for another way!

You just have to decide to change your future the way God wants you to do it. Bring Him seed that He can multiply, and then watch what happens as that seed grows into a harvest that turns your life around!

PRINCIPLES OF GIVING
TO CHANGE YOUR FUTURE

★ A Person of Excellence uses his seed to embrace God's future assignment.

★ A Person of Excellence understands that in order to obtain something he has never had, he has to do something he has never done.

★ The Excellent are aware that the laws of God are to be *obeyed* — not *discussed.*

★ A Person of Excellence depends upon his sowing to change his future.

★ The Excellent realize that reward will never be experienced in their lives until someone first recognizes their excellence.

★ A Person of Excellence understands that his faith pleases God only when it is accompanied by action.

★ Our destiny in life is completely determined by where we place our treasure.

★ A Person of Excellence knows that at times he must begin the flow of giving to release others into the abundance of God.

★ A bountiful future awaits those who continue to use their seed to create their future.

★ It is injustice in the courtroom of Heaven for a sower not to receive a harvest.

★ We are only rewarded for our *actions* and never for our *intentions.*

NOTES:

★★★★★

CHAPTER FOUR

SCRIPTURAL PRINCIPLES OF PROSPERITY

The law of sowing and reaping is definitely the "king-pin" to excellence in giving. But the Bible gives us many other guidelines as well concerning the financial realm in the life of a believer. I want to share just a few of these principles of prosperity that God has given us in His Word.

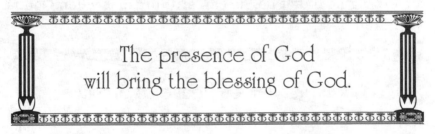

The presence of God
will bring the blessing of God.

God not only wants us to prosper, but according to Isaiah 48:17, He actually wants to teach us *how* to profit:

Thus says the Lord, your Redeemer, the Holy One of Israel: "I am the Lord your God, who teaches you to profit, who leads you by the way you should go."

Accordingly, you'll find that whenever the Bible says the Lord was with someone, that person prospered. In fact, this was one of the primary ways people could see that God was with a person.

Certainly this was true in the life of Joseph. Genesis 39:2 says, **"The Lord was with Joseph, and he was a successful man; and he was in the house of his master the Egyptian."**

According to this verse, a person can be a slave and still be a prosperous man! Now let's look at verse 23. At this time, Joseph was in jail after being unjustly accused of raping his master's wife.

> **The keeper of the prison did not look into anything that was under Joseph's authority, because the Lord was with him; and whatever he did, the Lord made it prosper.**

So even if someone has been thrown in prison for something he didn't do, he can still prosper when God is with him!

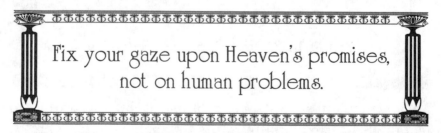

Fix your gaze upon Heaven's promises, not on human problems.

It is obvious that Joseph lived according to the truth found in that verse we looked at earlier: **"The blessing of the Lord makes one rich, and He adds no sorrow with it"** (Prov. 10:22). We need to do the same. Excellence won't come in our lives until we stop fixing our gaze on our problems. Those problems are just temporary, but the more we look at them, the more they'll gain control over our daily experience.

That's why we must refuse to dwell on every mental picture of defeat, past or present, and determine to fix our gaze on God's picture of prosperity that He's reserved for us. Only then will we begin to experience for ourselves what it means to have the blessing of the Lord make us rich.

Why do we prosper when our focus is on God? First, we start tapping into His wisdom. This helps us avoid making foolish decisions with our money that cause us to lose the increase God has blessed us with.

Second, God's desire to prosper us becomes more real to us than our need to prosper.

For instance, Romans 8:32 says, **"He who did not spare His own Son, but delivered Him up for us all, how shall He not with Him also freely give us all things?"** God says He will freely give us *all* things. As we get a revelation of "freely all things" in our hearts, we'll stop praying the problem: "Oh, Lord, where am I going to get the money? What am I going to do? Oh, Lord, please come through for me."

That kind of praying never gets us anywhere; in fact, it can make matters worse. But focusing on God *does* work — every time. Blessings and increase will begin to flow into our lives as we allow Him to teach us to profit in every situation.

Let me share another scripture that I focus on all the time:

For you know the grace of our Lord Jesus Christ, that though He was rich, yet for your sakes He became poor, that you through His poverty might become rich.

2 Corinthians 8:9

This is a great scripture to confess daily: "I know the grace of my Lord Jesus Christ, that though He was rich, yet for my sake He became poor so that I through His poverty will become rich." You can believe this statement because it isn't my opinion or someone else's opinion. *God* said it, so that's what you need to focus on. Be interested in what *God* thinks, not what anyone else thinks.

Third John 2 also says something about our need to focus our thoughts on God's promises instead of our problems:

Beloved, I pray that you may prosper in all things and be in health, just as your soul prospers.

God doesn't just want you to prosper; He wants you to prosper *in all things.* But notice what draws prosperity out from within you. The prerequisite to prosperity manifesting in your life is that *your soul* would prosper.

Once again, this means that you have to fix your mind on God's promises to prosper you rather than on the negative circumstances that may surround you. You have to hold this thought in your mind at all times: *Lord, You want to bless me so I can be a blessing. You want to bless me so I can be a blessing. You want to bless me so I can be a blessing.*

I learned to think like this years ago. I don't think about how I can be blessed because I already know what God thinks about that. He wants me to be greatly blessed so I can be a great blessing to others.

So how do we reach this place of "more than enough"? Here are a few more principles of prosperity we need to know in order to get there.

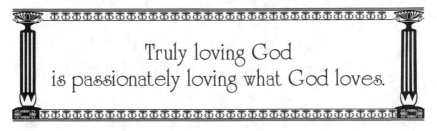

Truly loving God
is passionately loving what God loves.

If you want to prosper as God intends for you to prosper, discover what God is in love with; then determine to love the same thing too.

That's what Solomon did the night he asked for wisdom to rule God's people (2 Chron. 1:8-10). As we saw before, David had just gone home to be with the Lord, and now Solomon was taking his place. To get God's attention, Solomon offered a thousand burnt offerings to Him in one day. That night the Lord appeared to Solomon and asked, "What can I do for you?"

Right then Solomon made the decision to love what God loves. The young king replied, "Lord, I'm asking You for wisdom and knowledge so that I may lead this people of Yours. For who can lead so great a people as the people of God?"

After asking for divine wisdom, Solomon shut up. Why? Because he was thinking long term. He understood that in order to lead God's people, he'd need God's presence; he'd need money; he'd need to be seen as an able leader; and he'd need to have peace with his enemies. But first and foremost, Solomon knew he needed wisdom. That divine wisdom would help him obtain whatever else he needed as king.

Solomon understood this principle of prosperity:

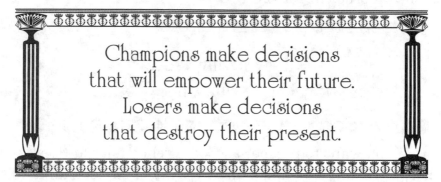

Champions make decisions
that will empower their future.
Losers make decisions
that destroy their present.

Solomon decided to choose long-term gratification. He thought, *I'm going to make a decision that will affect my future.* He already knew all it would take to be king; nevertheless, he said, "Lord, I'm only asking You for this one thing."

But notice what resulted from Solomon's prayer: He received everything else he needed when he made that one request, because he found out what God loves and determined to love it too.

Immediately God said, "Because you have not asked to prevail over your enemies, no enemy will oppose Israel in your lifetime. Because you have not asked for long life, you're going to live a long life. Because you haven't asked for wealth and riches and honor, I'm going to give you wealth and riches and honor until you are blessed beyond anyone who has come before you and all those who come after you. And I will also give you the wisdom and knowledge you've asked Me for so you can excel at leading My people."

You see, Solomon knew that inside his request was every bit of what God ultimately gave him — all because he decided to love what God loves.

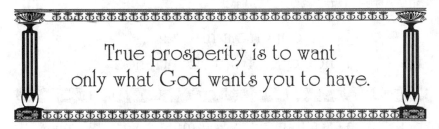

True prosperity is to want only what God wants you to have.

So many times people waste much of their lives pursuing things they shouldn't even have anything to do with — things that won't do them any good even after they've achieved their goal.

But we are to want what God wants for us. That's why Proverbs 30:8 (*NAS*) says, **"...Give me neither poverty nor riches; feed me with the food that is my portion."**

Notice that the writer *didn't* say, "Lord, give me riches." No, he said, "Give me the portion You have prepared for me."

What is *your* portion from the Lord? Someone might say, "Well, I prayed and asked God to give me the portion He has prepared for *me*, because what He gives to one person is different than what He gives to another. Maybe God wants me to make do with just a little so I become more spiritual."

But that isn't true. God has prescribed goodness and blessing for every one of us. However, the only way we can receive the fullness of God's goodness is to believe what His Word says and then to want only what He wants for us.

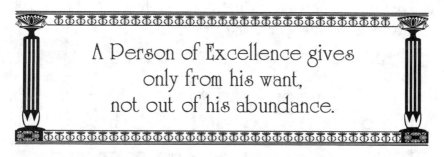

A Person of Excellence gives
only from his want,
not out of his abundance.

To be an excellent giver, you must give only from your want, never out of your abundance. That's what David did when he paid for the man's threshing floor in order to build an altar. David's foolishness had caused a plague to be released on the people of God; now he had to do whatever was necessary to stop that plague. So David dug a big hole into his want — his desire to see the plague stopped — and planted a seed; then he trusted in God to fill the hole back up again and bring in the harvest.

We saw another example of this principle in operation in Mark 12, which talks about the widow woman who put two mites — all the money she had — into the temple treasury. Before that, Jesus had watched many others give out of their abundance. But Jesus wasn't impressed with those people's offerings. However, He *was* impressed with the little woman who walked up to that offering container and put in the two mites that represented everything she had at the time.

Jesus called His disciples over and said, "Look at that woman. The other people all gave out of their abundance, but she gave all she had."

Let me stress an important point here: If you study the Word, you'll find that every time there was an offering, there was a specific reason for that offering. How does that apply to you? *When you sow a seed, you need to understand what you're sowing it for.*

The question is, what's *your* reason for sowing seed?

Some people say, "Well, I don't want anything."

I'm not talking to people who say that. The truth is, a person who doesn't think he wants anything should take a look at his salvation card and make sure it's been punched! How can anyone say that God doesn't have anything he or she wants?

Someone else might say, "Well, I don't need anything because I've been blessed with all spiritual blessings in the heavenly realms in Christ Jesus [Eph. 2:6]."

Yes, but how are you going to get the blessing you need from the heavenly realms into your pocket? Isn't that an example of something you want?

"Well, sure, that's something I want."

Then how are you going to get it? You're not going to receive the fullness of God's blessings with no cost or effort on your part. You have to make a big hole in the middle of your want and plant your seed there. And as you give from your want, your seed will eventually grow into a desire that has come to pass.

Let's go back to this widow woman for a moment. What was *her* want? She didn't have any money. She had nothing. So she cleared a place right in the middle of her want and then planted the seed she had — two mites — so it could grow into a multiplied harvest.

This principle works in every area of life, not just in the area of finances. For instance, do you need love? Then you need to give love out of your want for love. Whatever you need more of is what you need to give, because only when you *give* it do you set yourself in position to *receive* it. Forgive, and you'll be forgiven. Give, and it shall be given unto you. Whatever it is that you need, you first have to give it.

That's what this little lady did. She had a want; her want was money. So she sowed into her want all the money she had. (Notice that she sowed what she had, *not* what she didn't have.) And because this widow woman sowed such precious seed, she received back a multiplied harvest — not the least of which was Jesus' commendation when He said, "She has put in more than all of them."

Why did Jesus say that? Because none of the other people gave from their want, nor did they ever assign one of those seeds to a specific harvest. They just went to the temple courts in all their foolish pride and arrogance to make a show in front of people. They wanted other people to think big things about them. Only the little widow woman cooperated with God by sowing into her want.

That's why your seed needs to be sown into your want every time you tithe or give an offering. You should never just throw money into the offering bucket without assigning it to a specific harvest. You have to have inside your mind, *This is why I'm doing what I'm doing.* There has to be a reason for your gift if you are to receive any benefit from giving it.

"But I'm pretty content at the level I'm at."

That's why God wants you to sow — so you can be more abundantly blessed than everyone else around you and thus become the one who blesses others!

Personally, I don't go to work for myself any longer. I also don't owe anyone any money. Those days are over. They're finished! Now I go to work for what I can *give*, not for what I can *get*.

Are you at that place yet? You get there by giving from your want.

Let's say your home isn't paid for yet. You can choose to pursue the goal of getting that house paid for in less than half the time by giving from your want.

Why should you do that? Because until the time you pay off that mortgage, you're serving the mortgage company. Every day you're going to work so you can pay for something you don't own. You may think you own it, but in reality, someone is loaning that house to you.

Someone is letting you live there until it's paid for, as long as you pay a certain amount of money each month with interest. And in the end, you'll have paid $300,000 for a $100,000 house!

All of us need to live continually in a state of want. I sure do. I'm telling you, there are some *big* wants in my life. This is where I want to go. This is what I want to do. This is what I want to achieve. These are the friends I want to have. This is the future I want to build for my family. This is the direction I want to take my family — out of the socioeconomic life I've given them so far and up to a much higher level. Therefore, I have purposed that every time I sow, I will sow into my want, for whatever I sow in want, I will reap in joy.

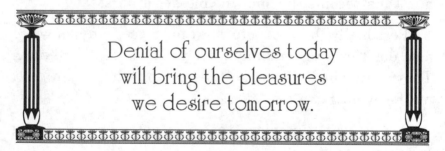

Denial of ourselves today
will bring the pleasures
we desire tomorrow.

The more I act upon these principles of giving I've been sharing with you, the more opportunities arise for me to choose to give again. And with each opportunity, I must also embrace self-denial in order to make the greater choice. Once more I have to put off into my future the gratification of reaping the reward of my harvest.

Nevertheless, that is the choice I make again and again and again. I keep refusing to cash in or to stop giving in this present moment. Instead, I choose to keep on sowing at every opportunity, putting off into the future my own personal gratification.

Most people want to receive gratification now and pay for the gratification later. However, they don't realize that they won't be able to pay in their latter years for all the things they are buying now. Their income-producing years are getting less every day; yet they just keep on spending money for their present gratification.

That's how God gets a bad reputation. The world says He doesn't take care of His kids because so many are trapped in heavy debt. No, God's kids made the mistake of adopting a "Wimpy mentality." I'm talking about those old Popeye cartoons where Wimpy always said, "I'll gladly pay you Tuesday for a hamburger today." So many Christians want to "eat their hamburger" today and pay for it on Tuesday. But just like Wimpy, they never have the money to pay what they owe on Tuesday either!

America is even worse than the rest of the world in this area of credit. As an American consumer, we can get credit anywhere. Many companies will even give us credit if we have filed for bankruptcy! So the pattern begins — we get more and more credit until debt becomes a trap that keeps us from moving forward in life. Soon our future is so entangled in debt that we're not even free to obey God's call on our lives.

All we have to do to avoid that sad situation is to *delay our gratification*. That doesn't mean we have to eat dried beans and hamburger all the time. We just have to delay our gratification into the future according to one determining factor: *that we choose to become like God in every situation to the best of our ability.*

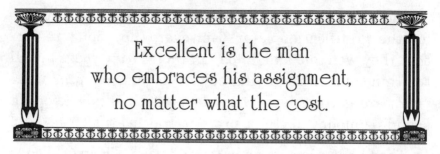

Excellent is the man
who embraces his assignment,
no matter what the cost.

First Chronicles 22:6-11 is the account of David charging Solomon with the task of building a house for God. David tells Solomon of the time he went to the Lord and said, "Lord, I live in a palace and You live in a tent. I want to build a magnificent house for You."

But God said to David, "No, you can't do that because you're a man of war. You have shed too much blood in your life. However, your son Solomon *will* build Me a house."

Notice there is no indication that David got upset when God told him that. I wonder what the reaction of most modern Christians would be if they said to the Lord, "Lord, I want to build You a house," and the Lord replied, "No, you won't be able to build Me a house, so your son will do it."

Most people probably wouldn't believe it was God speaking to them. They'd probably say, "I rebuke you, devil, in Jesus' Name!" Then they'd go off in a huff saying, "I'm going to build God a house, no matter what anyone says! I'll do what I want to do!"

But David didn't do that, nor did he get upset. In fact, David actually turned to the Lord and said in essence, "You may have told me that I couldn't build You a house, but You never told me I couldn't pay for it!" Then David turned to his son Solomon and said, "Here's all the money. Here's all the wood. Here's all the gold. Here's everything you'll ever need."

David was a person of excellence, so he just smiled and embraced the role God was allowing him to play. Even in the final days of his life here on this earth, David purposed to fulfill his assigned part in God's plan.

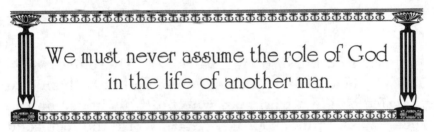

We must never assume the role of God in the life of another man.

We must never take God's place in someone else's life by serving as that person's provider through unscriptural means. For instance, Proverbs 6:1-3 (*TLB*) talks about the folly of cosigning a loan for someone:

> **Son, if you endorse a note for someone you hardly know, guaranteeing his debt, you are in serious trouble.**
>
> **You may have trapped yourself by your agreement.**
>
> **Quick! Get out of it if you possibly can! Swallow your pride; don't let embarrassment stand in the way. Go and beg to have your name erased.**

If you identify with this passage of Scripture — if you've ever cosigned a loan for someone else and wished you hadn't done that — here's why: There's always a reason that a person needs a cosigner in order to secure a loan to purchase something. God is trying to tell that person that it isn't time for him to obtain the material possession he's pursuing. God is saying, "Not now. Later on you'll be able to get that — when you can believe for it yourself."

The person who has asked you to help him secure a loan doesn't need *you* — he needs to believe *God* for his needs to be met. If you cosign for him, the Bible says you will be snared.

Jesus said in Matthew 7:24 (*NIV*), **"Therefore everyone who hears these words of mine and puts them into practice is like a wise man who built his house on the rock."** Well, think about it — God's Word, the rock-solid foundation we're supposed to build our lives on, has already told us, **"...If you become surety for your friend, if you have shaken hands in pledge for a stranger ...DELIVER YOURSELF..."** (Prov. 6:1,3).

What happens if we ignore God's instructions? Jesus went on in Matthew 7:26,27 (*NIV*) to tell us:

> **"But everyone who hears these words of mine and does not put them into practice is like a foolish man who built his house on sand.**
> **The rain came down, the streams rose, and the winds blew and beat against that house, and it fell with a great crash."**

If we hear what God is telling us to do but ignore His words, we can expect one thing to happen: Sooner or later, some area of our lives will fall with a great crash. Regarding this subject of cosigning a loan for someone, what often crashes is our relationship with the person we were trying to help!

God has already told you, "Don't become surety for anyone, not even your friend." Now it's up to you to make a commitment never to cosign for anyone. Lock in on that commitment and don't change for anyone, not even for Jesus Himself.

Someone might ask, "Do you mean you wouldn't change even if Jesus told you to change?"

No, and I'll tell you why. Jesus wouldn't tell me to change because He would never contradict His Father's Word.

So if you ever feel any pressure to become surety for someone else, rest assured that the pressure isn't coming from Jesus. If you hear a voice say, "This is the Lord speaking to you, and I'm telling you that you need to go and cosign for that person," you just tell him, "I rebuke you, devil, in Jesus' Name!" Jesus would never tell you to do that. He doesn't talk that way.

I can't imagine Jesus going over to Michael the archangel and saying, "Mike, I don't have enough to finish the pearly gates. Do you think we could break into your piggy bank? I know this is your retirement fund, Mike, but I really need your help." Nor can I imagine a memo going out to everyone in Heaven that says, "All paychecks are stopped until further notice while the

Father finishes His heavenly mansion." It just doesn't happen that way in Heaven, and it isn't supposed to happen that way in God's Kingdom here on earth!

You see, Jesus has plenty of money; He doesn't need you to cosign for anyone. If someone comes to you needing money, Jesus would rather provide you with the money to give to that person so you don't have to cosign for him.

Now, I know how it is sometimes. You love people, and you don't want to hurt them. So when someone comes to you, asking you to cosign a loan for him, you don't like to tell that person no. You want him to make it in life.

But instead of giving in and agreeing to do what God has told you not to do, just say, "You know, I love you, but I'm not going to cosign for you. I'll give you all the money I have to give. I know it's not as much as you need, but it's every penny I have. I never even want to see it again. If you ever give it back to me, I'll be happy. But if you never do, it won't affect our relationship at all. I'll just keep on loving you, no matter what."

If I ever even entertained the idea of loaning money to anyone, I'd only do it if I never expected a dime back from that person. I'd pay the debt myself before I'd ever call that person on the telephone and ask, "When are you going to be able to pay me back? Are you going to be able to pay me back? I just don't know what I'm going to do if you don't pay me back."

Why would I refuse to ask that person for the money he owes me? Because that would mean I was living my life in fear. It would also mean that I had set the stage for my relationship with that person to be destroyed, because the relationship would then be dependent on his paying me back. If he didn't pay me back, our relationship would be over. And if he did pay me back, he still might want to end his relationship with me for the way I treated him!

So if you're wondering if you should loan money to someone, ask yourself this: *Would it bother me if this person never paid back the money?* If you answer yes, don't loan him the money. Tell the person, "I want to preserve my relationship with you; therefore, I will not do it."

> We must never trade away our future to create a present season of comfort.

Do you realize that when you don't owe anyone any money, you can save money fast? Well, consider this — if you saved only a dollar a day, you'd be ahead of most Americans. But when you have all sorts of debts, it's difficult to save a dime.

I want you to understand that until you become resolute in your decision that God is the One who meets your needs, you will flounder in life, especially in the realm of finances. Therefore, this is my recommendation: Taking one step at a time, move a little closer each day to the decision that you'll never again put yourself in a situation where you have to borrow money. The moment you finally get to that place in life is the moment God can start really blessing you.

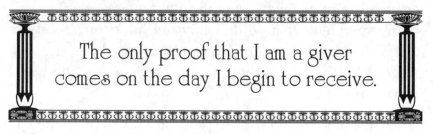

The only proof that I am a giver comes on the day I begin to receive.

Do you know how I find out whether or not I'm a giver? By looking at my checkbook.

Too many times Christians think that they're givers, but they haven't really given much at all. Someone once said to me, "I'm a giver, but nothing has been happening in my life."

I replied, "Well, let me help you with this. *The day you can know you're a giver is the day you begin to receive.*"

How can I say that with such confidence? Because I know what Jesus said in Luke 6:38:

> **"Give, and it will be given to you: good measure, pressed down, shaken together, and running over will be put into your bosom. For with the same measure that you use, it will be measured back to you."**

We need to be very careful, because every time we say, "Lord, I've been giving, but I'm not receiving," in effect we're calling Jesus a liar. After all, *He* is the One who said, "Give, and it *shall* be given to you."

So until I begin to receive, I can know that I have yet to ring God's bell. I haven't really become a giver in His eyes until increase begins to be given unto me.

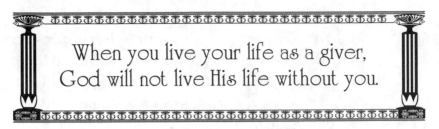

When you live your life as a giver,
God will not live His life without you.

This is the bottom line. God wants you to live your life as a giver. As you obey Him in this area of giving, He promises to live His life through you, making you a great blessing to everyone you meet.

That's the message in Second Corinthians 9:6,7 (*AMP*):

> [Remember] this: he who sows sparingly and grudgingly will also reap sparingly and grudgingly, and he who sows generously [that blessings may come to someone] will also reap generously and with blessings.
>
> Let each one [give] as he has made up his own mind and purposed in his heart, not reluctantly or sorrowfully or under compulsion, for God loves (He takes pleasure in, prizes above other things, and is unwilling to abandon or to do without) a cheerful (joyous, "prompt to do it" giver [whose heart is in his giving].

So determine to pursue excellence in giving at every turn. Look for opportunities to sow generously into your want and bless someone else in the process. As you live your life like this, you can know beyond a shadow of a doubt that you are on your way out of that socioeconomic box you've been stuck in for so long. Your financial situation is on the verge of a miraculous turnaround, for the harvest from the seed you've sown *must* come.

Take your eyes off what you don't have in the natural, and fix your gaze on God's promise to prosper you, knowing that God is unwilling to abandon or to do without you. In fact, He absolutely *must* have you in His life. After all, you are a cheerful, joyous, "prompt to do it" giver — just like Him!

PRINCIPLES OF PROSPERITY

* The presence of God will bring the blessing of God.

* Fix your gaze upon Heaven's promises, not on human problems.

* Truly loving God is passionately loving what God loves.

* Champions make decisions that will empower their future. Losers make decisions that destroy their present.

* True prosperity is to want only what God wants you to have.

* A Person of Excellence gives only from his want, not out of his abundance.

* Denial of ourselves today will bring the pleasures we desire tomorrow.

* Excellent is the man who embraces his assignment, no matter what the cost.

* We must never assume the role of God in the life of another man.

* We must never trade away our future to create a present season of comfort.

* The only proof that I am a giver comes on the day I begin to receive.

* When you live your life as a giver, God will not live His life without you.

NOTES:

CONFESSION OF FAITH
FOR AN EXCELLENT GIVER

I am an incurable seed-sower, and I don't want to be cured. I show love to everyone around me. I leave nothing unloved or untouched by my giving, for I know God blesses me so I can be a blessing.

I refuse to give anything to the Lord that costs me nothing. As I purpose to pursue Him every day of my life, I know that God is causing increase and prosperity to come to me. Because I love His wisdom, I excel in my work. I will stand before great men, not obscure men, because wisdom is the principal thing.

For my sake Jesus became poor so that through His poverty, I would become rich. I accept God at His Word and lay hold of His promises. As I choose to obey and serve Him every moment of my life, I will spend my days in prosperity and my years in pleasure!

PRAYER OF SALVATION

Perhaps you have never been born again and therefore haven't even begun the pursuit of excellence in God. If you have never received Jesus Christ as your personal Lord and Savior and would like to do that right now, just pray this simple prayer:

Dear Lord Jesus, I know that I am lost and need Your forgiveness. I believe that You died for me on the Cross and that God raised You from the dead. I now invite You to come into my heart to be my Lord and Savior. Forgive me of all sin in my life and make me who You want me to be. Amen.

If you prayed this prayer from your heart, congratulations! You have just changed your destiny and will spend eternity with God. Your sins were forgiven the moment you made Jesus the Lord of your life. Now God sees you as pure and holy, as if you had never sinned. You have been set free from the bondage of sin!

OTHER BOOKS
BY ROBB THOMPSON

Victory Over Fear

The Winning Decision

You Are Healed

Marriage From God's Perspective

The Great Exchange:
Your Thoughts for God's Thoughts

Winning the Heart of God

Shattered Dreams

Excellence in Ministry

Excellence in Attitude

Excellence in the Workplace

Excellence in Marriage

The Endless Pursuit of Excellence

For a complete listing of additional products
by Robb Thompson, please call:

1-877-WIN-LIFE
(1-877-946-5433)

You can also visit us on the web at:
www.winninginlife.org

God didn't call you to live a life of mediocrity.
He didn't create you to be "just good enough."

These books will guide you down the road to excellence
so that you can experience the extraordinary
and bask in God's best.
Make the quality decision to pursue
His standard of excellence in every area of your life!

The Endless Pursuit of Excellence
ROBB THOMPSON
$5   #4023

EXCELLENCE in the Workplace
ROBB THOMPSON
FOREWORD BY DR. MIKE MURDOCK
$15   #4020/Soft Cover
$24   #4022/Hard Cover

EXCELLENCE in Marriage
ROBB THOMPSON
$25   #4024/Hard Cover

Order Today!

Charge Orders, Call:
United States
1-800-622-0017
Europe
(+44) 0 1865-553-920

Europe Orders:
Winning in Life
Box 12
266 Banbeury Rd
Oxford OX27DL England

U.S. Orders:
Winning in Life
18500 92nd Avenue
Tinley Park, IL 60477

To contact Robb Thompson, please write:

Robb Thompson
P. O. Box 558009
Chicago, Illinois 60655

Please include your prayer requests
and comments when you write.